The Call

BOOKS BY ORIAH MOUNTAIN DREAMER

The Invitation

The Dance

The Call

Discovering Why You Are Here

ORIAH MOUNTAIN DREAMER

HarperSanFrancisco
A Division of HarperCollins*Publishers*

HarperCollins books may be purchased for educational, business, or sales promotional use. For information please write: Special Markets Department, HarperCollins Publishers, Inc., 10 East 53rd Street, New York, NY 10022.

HarperCollins Web site: http://www.harpercollins.com
HarperCollins®, ®, and HarperSanFrancisco™ are
trademarks of HarperCollins Publishers, Inc.
FIRST EDITION

Designed by Joseph Rutt

Library of Congress Cataloging-in-Publication Data
Mountain Dreamer, Oriah.
The call : discovering why you are here / Oriah Mountain Dreamer. — 1st ed.
p. cm.
ISBN 0–06–001194–7 (cloth: alk paper)
1. Spiritual life. I. Title.
BL624.M6759 2003
299'.93—dc21   2003050832

03 04 05 06 07   RRD (H)   10 9 8 7 6 5 4 3 2 1

For Jeff

Contents

The Call

I have heard it all my life,
A voice calling a name I recognized as my own.

Sometimes it comes as a soft-bellied whisper.
Sometimes it holds an edge of urgency.

But always it says: Wake up, my love. You are walking asleep.
There's no safety in that!

Remember what you are, and let this knowing
take you home to the Beloved with every breath.

Hold tenderly who you are, and let a deeper knowing
color the shape of your humanness.

There is nowhere to go. What you are looking for is right here.
Open the fist clenched in wanting and see what you already
hold in your hand.

There is no waiting for something to happen,
no point in the future to get to.
All you have ever longed for is here in this moment, right now.

You are wearing yourself out with all this searching.

Come home and rest.

How much longer can you live like this?
Your hungry spirit is gaunt, your heart stumbles. All this trying.
Give it up!

Let yourself be one of the God-mad,
faithful only to the Beauty you are.

Let the Lover pull you to your feet and hold you close,
dancing even when fear urges you to sit this one out.

Remember, there is one word you are here to say with your whole being.
When it finds you, give your life to it. Don't be tight-lipped and stingy.

Spend yourself completely on the saying.
Be one word in this great love poem we are writing together.

ORIAH MOUNTAIN DREAMER

One

The Call

I have heard it all my life,
A voice calling a name I recognized as my own.

*I*t comes most often just before I fall asleep. There on the edge of restful darkness, as the defenses of a sharp and demanding mind crumble just a little around the edges, forbidden thoughts and unwanted feelings make a bid for consciousness. It has come for years, not every night, but intermittently, when I close my eyes: an image on the back of my eyelids, unbidden and unwelcome, an image of my own wrists, slit and bleeding.

I know this isn't what you expect from someone who writes about the deepest longings of the heart and soul, someone who has asserted and believes that we are in our essential nature compassionate and capable of being fully present. It's not what you expect from someone whose life is filled with meaningful work she enjoys, intimate relationships she values, and a commitment to cultivating a daily connection to the Sacred Mystery that is larger than herself.

It's not what I expect. But there it is. Most often in the image, my hands are completely cut off.

When this image first came to me years ago I would pull away from it quickly, afraid of what it might mean. Although I was not consciously feeling suicidal, I was afraid that perhaps on some level I was being drawn to consider suicide without even knowing it. I have counseled adults struggling with the lifelong wounding brought about by a parent's suicide. I have two sons I love. I did not want to give any ground to the thoughts or feelings I feared might be behind this image. Suicide was not and never will be an option.

But still the image comes, frequently but irregularly, like some strange and persistent messenger who will not give up until the message has been received. I decide to pay attention to what is happening in my life and the world when the image appears. I discover that the image does not come more frequently when things in the world seem to be falling apart at an accelerated rate. The tragic events of September 11, the increased violence in the Middle East, stories of poverty and injustice within my own community all touch me deeply, but they do not alter how often or how vividly the image comes to me as I drift off to sleep. Neither does it seem to come with increased frequency when things in my own life are not going well. Sometimes the image appears when everything seems to be working out the way I want it to or think it should.

After years of being unable to banish the image, I finally decide to listen to what it has to tell me, to allow and be with the feelings that come when I simply stay with it. And I am flooded with a level of exhaustion that forces me to lie down on the bedroom floor next to my meditation cushion. The woman with her hands—a symbol of doing—severed says to me silently but emphatically, "I quit!"

I lie on the floor and consider the white plaster of the ceiling, allowing the feelings of failure to come. I stay with the knowledge of how frequently I am not fully present despite my intentions and my practice of meditation and prayer. I am frustrated at learning primarily in hindsight. During my contemplative meditation I can see clearly that I could have remained calm and compassionate when the woman from the insurance company informed me that my driving rating has been lowered and my premiums upped despite the fact that I did not make the claim or the police report that someone has apparently inserted into my file. But this insight was not available, did not guide me when I was speaking directly to her and she refused to correct the error. I am demoralized by how often I still find myself overtired from doing too much despite my efforts to increase my awareness of my own limitations by diligently doing my daily practice and conscientiously avoiding those things I know speed me up and make it harder to stay connected with myself and others—caffeine, TV, junk food. Over and over I resolve to slow down. And I do. I reorganize, take on less, let go of things that do not need to be done.

But the eyes of the woman in the image—my eyes—mirror the sense of futility that is growing within me, question the reason for all this effort, point to a hopelessness I just barely outrun each day. Her weary face dares to ask the question *why?* Why do any of it? Why not simply forget about being awake? Why not just find a really good pharmaceutical product that will allow me to continue to function in the world and be a happy carrot? What's the point of all this effort, all this diligent trying that seems to fail more often than it succeeds in creating awareness?

This is a story of my quest to hear and heed the call at the center of my life, the call to live the meaning—the why—at the center of all of our lives. It is an invitation to you to turn your attention to the call at the center of your life so that together we might begin to live consciously who and what we are and in so doing alleviate suffering in our lives and in the world and embody the deep happiness that is our birthright. The call is that consistent tug we feel at the center of our lives to do more than just continue, to know and fulfill the meaning of our lives. The call is always there, whispering in the soft places of our bodies and hearts, in the longing that reminds us what we ache for at the deepest level.

A year ago a dear friend, celebrating the changes in my work life, the steady book sales and opportunities to speak to different groups, said, "Oh, isn't it wonderful? It's what you always wanted, and it's all coming true!"

Later that night, at home in my bed, grateful for the opportunities that have come into my life but aware that these were never goals I consciously held or pursued, I see again the image of myself with severed hands, and I whisper into the darkness, "All I ever wanted was God."

I am neither a priest nor a theologian, neither a devotee of nor a spokesperson for any particular spiritual tradition or path. I am an ordinary woman with an extraordinary hunger: to live with an awareness of the Sacred Mystery, the Beloved—God—at the center of my life and to learn from this presence who I am and why I am here.

Speaking to me through *what* I long for, the call of that which is both within and larger than myself has guided me to an understanding of *how* I can live that longing—not by trying to change myself, but by unfolding, by becoming who I already am at the deepest level of my being. But with this comprehension of what I must do, the call continues to come to me as an image of myself with tired eyes and severed hands questioning *why* I seek to embody this understanding when it is clear how infrequently my essential nature guides my actions, how often fear still shapes and sometimes determines what I do. It tells me that something is off, missing. But I have not given up. I am willing to do whatever it takes to know and live the meaning in my life. I am convinced that I have to and am able to learn to *do* it differently.

And I am wrong.

Not knowing I am wrong, in the summer of 2002 I decide to go into the wilderness alone to do a forty-day vision quest, a ceremonial time of fasting, praying, and deep listening found in different forms in many spiritual traditions. Over the past eighteen years I have done eight personal vision quests, some for one to four nights and one for twenty-two days and nights. I am feeling strong, prepared, and cautiously optimistic.

I am lying facedown in the dirt and pine needles, waiting for the sharp pains in my belly to soften and ebb away. For the third time in as many hours I have vomited onto the ground the small sips of water I keep swallowing in an effort to stay hydrated. It has been twenty-four hours since I have been able to keep anything, including water, down. Trying to eat small bites of an apple hours before was like trying to swallow razor blades. I can feel the rapid fluttering of my heartbeat behind the steady throbbing in my head. When I roll over the whole world, a dizzying swirl of rocks and ground and leaves and sky, rolls with me and keeps on rolling even when I have stopped. It takes several minutes for my view of the gray sky above the tops of the trees that surround me to stabilize. The nausea and aching muscles have made sleeping difficult. I have been awake for almost forty-eight hours.

I have been alone in the wilderness for six days. Because I plan to stay for forty days I am not fasting continuously. Half of the time I am eating one light meal per day of a quarter cup of rice, one vegetable protein patty, and one apple. The other half of the time, for three-day periods, I am water-fasting. Feeling ill took me by surprise on day four after only eight hours of water fasting. The severity and suddenness of my symptoms remain a mystery. I have fasted many times for much longer periods with much less preparation and experienced no physical repercussions. Several years earlier I water-fasted during a twenty-two-day quest with no ill effects. Having had chronic fatigue syndrome many years ago, I generally keep a close watch on my overall health and can anticipate and usually avoid any major immune system crashes by resting and using herbs and supplements. I'd arrived for this quest rested and healthy. The weather and the animals have been gentle. There is no apparent reason for being so sick.

I lie on my back and stare at the clouds, wondering how long I can manage to keep going without water. Constant dizziness makes movement difficult. Purple bruises and welts from staggering into trees and falling to the ground while gathering firewood cover my legs and arms. Having discovered a thermometer in my Adventure Medical Kit, I know I have a low-grade fever of about 100.5 degrees. I can feel tears gathering behind my eyes, but I know crying will make my already pounding headache feel like it's going to explode, so I swallow hard and, without any hope of an answer, speak out loud.

"Now what?"

And I hear a voice, the voice of one of the old women I have seen many times in my dreams and have come to call the Grandmothers. The voice says quietly, simply, "Go home."

I hold my breath, listening for more. Anger flashes through me. Is this a test to see if I'm sincere in my intention to be here for forty days? Are they trying to measure the depth of the desire I have poured into my prayers? Seeing me struggle with physical discomfort, are they testing my resolve, trying to tempt me into giving up? The tears I would not allow as an expression of discouragement come now as outrage, hot on my face. My words are choked out from behind clenched teeth: "Don't fuck with me!"

The voice comes again, slower, sadder, and impossibly softer, a breeze rippling through the maple leaves above me. "Oriah, go home."

And I break. I roll over and press my face into the earth, sobbing. How can I go home without an answer? I want to know how to do it differently, how to let the love I know is within me guide me when I am tired and impatient and judgmental with those around me. I think of them now, the people I love: my two beautiful sons, Nathan and Brendan, now young men of nineteen and twenty-two, both beginning their studies at university; Jeff, the man I am about to marry, who despite not really understanding what I am doing out here helped me pack in my supplies and waits for my return; my parents, restraining themselves from expressing their concern for their crazy daughter who, just before her forty-eighth birthday, has gone out into the wilderness for six weeks alone; the friends and students who have supported me, the many people who are praying for me. Is telling me to go home the Grandmothers' way of telling me I simply can't do it, I can't live differently, I can't live fully present with a deep sense of connection to myself and the Sacred Mystery guiding me all the time?

I raise my head off the ground.

"I'm not going home. I want . . . to know how . . . to do it differently. And I am willing to do whatever it takes!" This last declaration is fierce, desperate. For a few moments there is nothing but the silence of the forest.

"You can't get there from here, Oriah."

"What?!"

"What you are looking for cannot be bought by ordeal."

I sit up slowly, bewildered. I'm not trying to buy anything, am I? There is an element of ordeal in doing a vision quest: the fasting, the solitude, the physical rigors of living outdoors in the wilderness for an extended time in all kinds of weather, the bugs. But these are part of the process I know and trust, part of what has worked in the past to break down my resistance to seeing what I need to see, hearing what I need to hear. I live in a culture that glorifies the easy answer, packages and sells the promise of a quick fix. I am willing to sacrifice comfort for what matters, for what is real.

"What you are looking for cannot be earned or paid for with suffering or hard work. It is a gift. Grace. It can only be received."

A wave of hopelessness washes through me. I know how to try harder, work longer, suffer through. I'm good at it, and I am willing to do it. And they are telling me that not only is this not what is required but that it simply won't work.

"Try easier."

"I don't know how to do easy," I whisper. "And I don't trust people who do." This is a revelation I realize is true as soon as I say it. I trust others who, like me, trust hard work, assume it is required, dive into it willingly and do it well. "Give me something else to do. Anything. But don't ask me to do easier. I don't know how. I don't think I can. There must be something else." I am begging now, desperate to know that the answer to all my questions is not the one thing I truly feel I cannot do. I lie back down defeated, letting the tears slip silently out of the corners of my eyes and run down into my ears.

Finally the voice of the Grandmother comes again, softly, sadly. "You keep fighting with reality, Oriah. It's a losing battle. Give it up."

It is late in the day. Because the sky is overcast I cannot tell how close the sun is to setting. Not wanting to get caught in the dark on my way out of the bush, I resolve to wait until morning, reasoning that a good night's sleep may make staying possible or leaving safer.

Lying in my small tent later that night, I breathe through the nausea and dizziness, focusing on relaxing into the ache that runs through my arms and legs. I give up hoping for sleep and try to let the darkness be my rest. I continue to be unable to eat or drink anything without vomiting. At first light I sit up and do my morning prayers, asking for help in getting out of the wilderness. Getting into my canoe, I paddle across the lake. Already the air is warm and thick with humidity, the lake a sheet of gray glass under cloudy skies. The dense bush around me is silent, still. I am not pondering the meaning of following the Grandmother's directive to go home. I am focused on getting out. Strangely, I feel more stable in the canoe than I do on land. The hike along a trail to the nearby outfitters normally takes about twenty minutes, but each time I take a dozen steps I have to go down on my hands and knees and wait for my rapidly beating heart to return to normal and for the dizziness and nausea to recede.

I want to lie down on the path and wait for someone to find me and carry me out. We have set up a system of signal flags for safety, and I know that sooner or later today someone will come down the path from the outfitters so they can see the flag I have put up on the far side of the lake. Only two things keep me going: the knowledge that it could be twelve more hours before someone comes to check the flag, and the bugs. Every time I go down to the ground I am swarmed. A cloud of mosquitoes and deerflies descends and mercilessly bites at my head, neck, hands, and face, leaving large bloody welts. I grew up in northern Ontario, two hundred miles north of this wilderness site. I have camped and canoed for years, and yet I have never experienced bugs like this. They are relentless. I cannot breathe without inhaling insect bodies. The only way to keep from going completely mad from the buzzing and biting is to keep moving. As I stagger to my feet, it occurs to me that my prayer for help in getting out of the bush has been answered. The deerflies and mosquitoes ensure I will keep moving.

"I didn't mean by torturing me," I mutter. "I meant maybe having someone in an ATV (an all-terrain vehicle, which I normally detest for its noise and polluting exhaust) come along and give me a ride." I focus on taking the next step.

Two and a half hours later I stagger through a door into a scene that makes me wonder if I am dreaming or losing my mind. The long tables in the dining room of this remote northern outfitter are filled with Tibetan Buddhist monks eating breakfast. Startled, they look up from their porridge bowls as I stumble in. I must be quite a sight as I clump across the floor in my hiking boots to lean panting against the door frame. A large hunting knife hangs at my belt; my clothes are stuck to my body with sweat and covered in dirt. I have removed my hat to reveal hair plastered to my head with a week's worth of greasy and ineffective insect repellent. Out of the crowd of round faces and burgundy robes, Martha, one of the owners of the outfitters, emerges and moves toward me, her face filled with concern.

As unlikely as it seems, the Tibetan monks have traveled from India and are there to do ceremonial sand painting, meditation, and prayer. With the sound of their music and chanting in the background, I am taken care of tenderly, given food and water that miraculously stays down, and put to bed in a nearby cabin. Jeff is called and drives up, paddles in, packs my supplies, and with help from folks at the outfitters hauls them out of the bush.

And perhaps for the first time in my life I heed the call, the one I have heard all my life, and I go home.

This is a story about surrendering from a woman who has found surrender impossible. This is a story about stopping the war, my war, the one I have fought all my life, the one I have not been able to give up despite the fact that I have lost every battle and sincerely declared myself out of action over and over again. It's a story about stopping the war with what is within and around me because I have simply had enough of fighting, because I love my life and the world and have come to realize that in order to find the rest I ache for and the peace I want us to create together, I must give up the war I fight every time I allow my desire to create change, inner or outer, pull me into doing. Change will happen, change does happen, often as a result of our choices and our actions. But every time I let my actions be dictated solely or primarily by the desire to create change, every time I am attached to achieving a desired result, no matter how lofty or "spiritual" that hoped-for result may be, I am rejecting what is and so causing suffering in myself and in the world.

I thought that to heed the call, to know and embody the meaning of my life, I had to learn to do it differently. But what I had to learn, what I am still learning, was to stop doing altogether. I had to learn not-doing, something I had heard about years ago but dismissed as being at best an ideal beyond my humanness or at worst empty spiritual jargon. I remember the first time I heard a teacher, a Native American elder, tell a group of students that they had to learn the art of not-doing. I was a single mother with two small sons living on very little income, and I wondered just how not-doing would work when there are children to get up and dressed, breakfasts to prepare, lunches to pack, laundry to do, and a wage to be earned. I misunderstood. I assumed not-doing meant doing nothing—staring at a wall or sleeping—and there was precious little time for this in my life. Of course, even when we sit and stare at a wall or lie in bed sleeping we are usually doing something. We are thinking and feeling and sensing, if only in our dreams.

But not-doing does not depend on whether or not my body is moving or my mind is active. Not-doing is about letting any movement flow from an awareness of the deep and ever-present stillness that is what I am at the most essential level of being. It is here, in the awareness of my essential nature, that I find the meaning I seek in my life, not as an idea or an ideal but as an implicit knowing folded into my very being.

But without experience these are empty concepts, ideas lacking reality, and words are limited in describing that which is beyond thought and so beyond language. Lao-tzu in the *Tao-te Ching* wrote, *The way that can be told is not the eternal Way. The name that can be named is not the eternal Name.* But that does not stop us from sharing with words, however inadequate they might be, what we have learned and experienced. I write in the hope of discovering and sharing the truth at the center of our lives, a truth that is sometimes revealed only when the story is told, when we reach to articulate what has been learned.

What I have discovered by following the call to consciously discover and live the meaning in my life is not something unique or new. It echoes the experiences and insights of seekers and students and teachers on many different spiritual paths. Sometimes, when I write in my journal of some insight I have had into my own experience, I realize that it is familiar, similar or identical to something I have read or heard from a spiritual teacher. And I laugh at my own sense of discovery. One morning, shaking my head at the length of my journey to discover the truth in something I had been told years before, I think to myself, "Does each of us have to reinvent the wheel?" Even as the question comes I know the answer is yes. Yes, each of us needs to experience the truth for ourselves, each of us needs to follow our own path to self-realization even though the self we realize is in essence identical to and not truly separate from all others. There is simply no way to get there except by going through the process yourself.

This doesn't mean that teachers cannot be helpful, that we cannot learn from each other's stories. As the thirteenth-century Sufi mystic and poet Rumi wrote,

> *A story is like the water you heat for your bath.*
> *It takes messages between the fire and your skin.*
> *It lets them meet, and it cleans you.*

Stories honestly told and deeply contemplated offer us a glimpse of the meaning in our lives and give us insights into how we can consciously live this meaning. This is why I read and write: to find and share the messages that come from the fire of living.

I have studied many spiritual traditions and learned from many teachers, although I have had no one teacher as my primary guide. Perhaps my story has progressed slower as a result. Guidance has come to me in night dreams, in meditations, and during the ceremonies I was taught by Native American elders. As a child it came as a presence I took to be the God I heard about in my

Sunday school class, and later, from the time I was thirty, it also came as the image and voices of a circle of old women, the Grandmothers in my dreams. This has been my way. This is not an argument against working with a particular teacher or following the prescribed practices of an established tradition. Such structure, support, and guidance can be invaluable.

Your story will be different because the particulars of your history and your personality—the things that have shaped how and why you fight your war with reality and therefore how you stop the war—will be different from mine. But if you suffer at all for the world or yourself, if you spend one moment resenting, resisting, trying to hang onto, or deeply desiring to change what is within yourself or in the world right now, you are fighting with reality. And, as the Grandmothers have told me, fighting reality—even or perhaps especially the reality of who and what you are—is a losing battle.

In the end we all hear the same call to stop the war, and each of us decides if we will heed the voice that calls the name we recognize as our own. Some expect the call to come as a voice emanating from a flash of brilliant white light or in a vision surrounded by a golden glow. And sometimes it does. But sometimes it comes in a way that makes it hard to want to listen and harder yet to ignore. Sometimes it comes as an image of a woman I recognize standing alone, her shoulders rounded, her face etched with a tired sadness, her hands severed. But always it comes, this sacred life force calling to us, asking us to remember why we are here. We were programmed from the beginning to hear it, to feel the longing to go home to what we are, to quit trying to be other than we are, to learn how to stop our doing and surrender to simply being and so find the peace and the meaning embedded in our lives. It is the very nature of the stuff of which we are made, the impulse of the life force within us, to want to wake up and consciously embody that meaning.

It's what we are called to be. It's why we are here.

Meditation on Ending the War with Reality

Where are you fighting reality? In this meditation, allow whatever insights come in response to the questions to simply be there without judgment. Where do you long to stop doing?

Sit in a comfortable position and take three deep breaths, allowing your body to relax, letting go of any stress or tension on each exhale. Feel your body drop down. Let yourself be supported by the chair or cushion you are sitting upon, the floor beneath you, and the earth beneath the place where you sit. Let your shoulders drop down. Allow your weight to settle down into your hips and legs. Allow any thoughts or feelings or sensations that come to simply float away, neither clinging to nor resisting them. Bring your attention to your breath, and allow yourself to rest.

Allow the question to come, slowly and clearly: Where do I find myself struggling with what is? Where do I want to stop this struggle? Let the response begin with "I quit . . ." or "I stop struggling with . . ." and let it come, slowly and clearly, from a place of deep stillness. Do not judge what comes. If you begin to examine or analyze what comes, just allow these thoughts to drift away, and returning to your breath, begin once again to complete the phrase "I quit . . ." or "I stop struggling with . . ." When this process feels complete, bring your attention once again to your breath and sit quietly with the feeling and the sound of your inhale and your exhale.

Allow the question to come, slowly and clearly: Where do I fight reality? Let the response come in its own time from a place of deep stillness. There can be no right or wrong answer. Allow yourself to complete the phrase "I don't like . . ." or "I resent . . ." or "I resist . . .," letting images of situations in your life or the world come to you. Allow the fullness of your wanting things to be different than they are come into your awareness. Be with your own resistance to the way things are, feeling the tension it creates in your body, the suffering it creates in your mind and heart, breathing through the emotions and sensations that come.

Bring your attention back to your breath and let your shoulders drop. On each exhale tell yourself to simply "let it be," seeing in your mind's eye the situation you do not like or are resenting or resisting. Feel the resistance in your body flow out with the exhale. If it feels appropriate you may wish to complete the phrase "I end my war with . . . ," naming the situation you have struggled to accept as simply what is.

Two

Voice of the Beloved

◦────

Sometimes it comes as a soft-bellied whisper.
Sometimes it holds an edge of urgency.

But always it says: Wake up, my love. You are walking asleep.
There's no safety in that!

I remember the sound of my mother's voice calling my name. The sun is going down. The shadow of our house reaches out now and crosses the small rectangle of grass that is our front yard, edging into the street, turning the gray asphalt black. Lights from the windows of the houses that line the street glow yellow like cats' eyes in the dark. Although the blistering heat of a midsummer day has given way at last to the coolness of twilight, the houses still hold the hot sticky air of the day so we are allowed to stay outside a little longer than usual. We run through the adjoining backyards, a pack of small boys and girls excited by the unfamiliarity of our neighborhood in the fading light. There's a hint of danger in roaming about as darkness descends. Our voices seem to carry farther, and the familiar landscape of backyard sandboxes and broad front porches, barely visible now in the deepening shadows beneath the maples and oaks that line the street, seems suddenly more exotic and mysterious than the place we had grown bored with only hours before. We become feral beings running in the dark, feeling the rush and relief of cool air on bare limbs, scaring ourselves a little with high-pitched squeals and small screams.

Unexpectedly, this break with our usual routine of being in before sunset has given us a glimpse of a bigger world. We can taste the world's largeness and our own smallness, and because we know where home is, we can revel in the tingle of fear that runs through us. We can hear the voice that calls us, and we know that we will return to the place of belonging when it is time, and we know that if we fail to return the one who calls our name will come to look for us and take us home.

This is what it is like to live your life knowing you belong to something larger, something that is both around you in all that is and within you as the essence of what you are. To live with awareness of your essence is to sit in the center of silently knowing why you are here. You go out into the world, and sometimes the world breaks your heart, wounds your body, and overcomes your mind's ability to make sense of it all. But if you can stay aware of your own still center, if you can hear the sound of the voice of that which is larger than yourself—the Beloved—calling you home, you can meet the challenges, sometimes even revel in them, because you know where home is and you know you have not been forgotten.

My parents had one ironclad rule: when my brother or I heard one of them call our name, we had to answer. Even if we could not come right away because we were involved in the intricacies of some complex game, we had to answer, had to let my mother or father know that we had heard and that we were safe. We had to respond. The call of that which is larger than ourselves and yet not separate from us not only guides us home but asks for a response, reminds us that the world needs us awake.

Going home, leaving my vision quest site and returning to the city, wasn't as hard as I thought it would be although it did push me up against some thwarted and unacknowledged spiritual ambition. There is a certain audacity in going out into the wilderness and asking for guidance in living one small human life, although in all fairness I knew from past experience that I could count on the realities of fasting alone in the bug-ridden wilderness to subdue any idealized fantasies I might have of questing. Still, there were moments before the quest when I am sure I imagined myself emerging after forty days shimmering with the light of realization and emanating peace and wisdom to everyone. At the very least I wanted a good story to share when I came back, and a story of seven days in the bush is not nearly as impressive as a story of forty days. But I was happy to discover that I wanted an answer to my question—wanted to know the truth about how to live my life— more than I wanted to look good questing or have an entertaining story to tell later.

Part of what made it easy to leave was the severity and suddenness of my physical symptoms. Sometimes, when we ask to hear the call but are having trouble listening, the volume gets turned up. Staying could have created a serious health risk, and I was happy to confirm that I was not suicidal. The inexplicable pain in my body seemed to reinforce the message I had received just before I became ill. As I came out of a dream on my third night in the wilderness I heard a calm and steady voice saying, "Right path, Oriah. Wrong direction." I am not suggesting that vision questing isn't a useful and powerful way to seek guidance. Vision quests have proved invaluable to me and many others, and this one was no exception. The learning just didn't follow the course I thought it would. It rarely does.

The decision to go home was made easier because I trust the Grandmothers even though I cannot say with certainty who they are. Some people have claimed to know that the Grandmothers are simply a manifestation of my own inner wisdom speaking to me. Others have told me with mystifying certainty that the Grandmothers are ancestor spirit guides or enlightened teachers, beings that live in a different dimensional reality. Either way, their words and their presence hold the same deep and dynamic stillness I recognize as the essence of which all things are made. The Grandmothers are one of the ways that the Sacred Mystery that is both what I am and that which is larger than myself speaks to me.

It is perhaps not surprising, given my personal history of studying with Native elders and exploring feminine spirituality, that the sacred presence that is within and around us would appear in my dreams as a circle of wise old women. But if I had to guess at the core reason behind this image, I would credit my mother's mother, my own grandmother Nana. Nana was a sharp-eyed and sharper-tongued woman, barely four feet eleven inches tall. The eldest of nine children, she had left school early to get a job so she could help support her family, a hard sacrifice for a girl who, like me, loved books. A woman with strong ideas about what was right and wrong, Nana could put anyone in their place with a piercing look and the determined set of her thin lips. But to me she was the woman who thought I was beautiful. Unsure, as we all sometimes are, of my worth in the world, I remember feeling wonder at the way Nana tenderly stroked my cheek, telling me how beautiful I was. For some reason—perhaps because soft words did not frequently come from this small fierce woman—I believed her. I knew she truly saw me as beautiful, inside and out, and she loved the beauty she saw.

The night of my grandfather's death I went to my grandparents' home and stayed the night. My parents were upstairs in the master bedroom, my grandmother had bedded down on the living room sofa, and I slept in a single bed in the small room off the kitchen. Newly pregnant with my first child and exhausted by the day's events, I was sleeping soundly when the sound of someone entering the room startled me awake in the middle of the night. "Nana?" I whispered, but she did not answer. Ghostly in her pale flannel nightgown, she silently lifted the covers and slid into the narrow bed next to me, her small body trembling with cold and grief. Crying softly, she reached out and squeezed my hand, hard. For a moment I couldn't make any sense of it. This was not the grandmother I knew, the perpetual pillar of strength, a force to be reckoned with. This was a woman alone and lost without the husband she had loved for over fifty years. Rolling onto my side, I stroked her cheek as we talked quietly about my grandfather. The tips of my fingers still remember her soft skin, covered with lines of age, damp from tears. I had not noticed those lines in the daylight. Shocked at seeing my grandmother broken by something life had thrown at her, I could not find the words to tell her what I hoped my touch would: you are beautiful, and you are loved.

There are infinite ways for the call to reach us, and when it does, what it has to say may be challenging but it is never harsh. That which is larger than ourselves longs for us even as we long to know the continuous and sacred presence that holds and sustains it all. We are the Beloved's love. My friend Mark Kelso, a gifted musician and composer, writes in the lyrics of one of his songs, *We are loved more than we ever will know.* Each time I hear this my breath catches and I feel a small ache in the center of my chest for all the suffering caused by forgetting that this is so. However the call has come to me—whether as a disturbing image of a desperate self, the voices of the Grandmothers moving on the wind through the high branches of the trees, or in the love between me and those around me—even when the call asks me to risk something, asks me to do something that does not come easily, it is always tender, always calling me out of suffering and into greater joy.

Daniel Ladinsky, translator of the wonderful poetry of the Sufi mystic Hafiz, has translated and edited a book entitled *Love Poems from God.* Drawing on the writings of twelve spiritual poets from both Eastern and Western traditions, Ladinsky offers us the words of men and women who have experienced directly how much we are loved, how constantly the Beloved calls our name, how deeply God longs for us to wake up and know what we are and why we are here so that we might celebrate and participate fully in the joy and beauty of life. Always ecstatic and often erotic, these poems remind us of what we already know but often cannot seem to remember: that all things are an expression of the Sacred Mystery that woos us away from our suffering. Meister Eckhart, the German Catholic theologian and mystic of the early fourteenth century, writes, in Ladinsky's collection,

> *How long will grown men and women in this world*
> *keep drawing in their coloring books*
> *an image of God that*
> *makes them*
> *sad?*

Gently he admonishes,

> *It is a lie—any talk of God*
> *that does not*
> *comfort*
> *you.*

Why is it so hard for us to hear the voice of the Beloved calling our name? Why is it so easy for us to believe that we have been forgotten, that the call may come for others but not for us? Years ago, family and friends gathered at a summer cottage and played a game that involves guessing the meaning of words. Someone offered the word *oubliette*. Only my younger son, Nathan, proficient player of the apparently educational role-playing video games, knew that it is a kind of dungeon with only one opening in the high ceiling, a prison from which there is simply no escape without assistance from the outside. The dictionary etymology of the word described it as meaning "a place where one is forgotten." When I read this aloud, there were short involuntary gasps from the adults in the room. We heard in that bleak phrase the human experience—our own experience—of despair.

To feel that you are forgotten—not to hear something call your name as the darkness descends—this is the worst of what we all fear.

We are never forgotten, always called, but sometimes old wounds make it hard for us to hear, hard for us to sit still and listen. There were children in my neighborhood all those years ago for whom being out after dark on a warm summer night was normal. No one at home knew where they were or seemed to care. No one ever called their name or waited anxiously for them to respond. They were mystified at the excitement we felt at being out on our own in the dark. For them, roaming around in the fading light was just another moment of being continually on their own, and the place they called home was not necessarily a place of refuge or belonging. They did not flirt with fear and return to safety. What fears they had were too real, too likely to be realized. They were survivors and knew about a kind of courage I would not have to learn for years.

Sometimes we are afraid that if we are still nothing will ever call to us, that we will be left standing there feeling foolish and abandoned, exposed as someone who dared to think themselves worthy of being called.

Attending a writing retreat in upstate New York, I find myself unable to write and disappointed with the instructions and demeanor of the workshop facilitator. As always happens, rejecting what is causes my body to tense. By the end of my second day at the retreat, my neck and shoulders are a mass of knotted muscles and my shoulder blades feel like they have been embedded in concrete. Getting up from my chair, I turn and feel the left side of my back go into a deep and painful spasm. I shuffle to the health clinic on-site where massage therapists offer treatments, only to find there are no appointments available. Unable to sit or even lie down comfortably and hoping to distract myself from my mental fuming and physical discomfort, I decide to observe a workshop promising to demonstrate something called Contemplative Dance.

The workshop is led by Daphne Lowell, a tall elegant woman about my age who is moving with considerably more grace and agility than I display at my best moments. She invites us to sit or stand slightly away from others anywhere in the spacious room. I hobble over to a corner, awkwardly sliding down the wall to sit on the polished wooden floor, intending to watch the others and move as little as possible. Daphne invites us to close our eyes and follow the breath as it moves in and out of our bodies. Even in my disabled state I figure I can do this, although my breaths are shallow as I try to avoid the sharp ache that moves through my back if I expand my rib cage fully. Daphne keeps telling us that what we are about to do we simply cannot do wrong. How we are breathing right now is fine, whatever movement comes will be the right movement. She guides us in focusing on our bodies—the skin, the extremities, the musculature, the bones—her soft voice taking us deeper and deeper into an awareness of our bodies. Lightly tapping a steady rhythm on a large polished gourd, she moves around the room, inviting us to move if and when the impulse to move comes from deep within our own bodies, allowing that impulse to guide the speed and shape of our movement. Gently she warns us against going into any automatic sequence of motions that might arise from familiar exercise routines. We are told again and again to move only as quickly as we can stay connected to the impulse to move, to stop if we lose the thread of that impulse and wait in stillness until the movement again comes from deep within. The movement is less important than staying connected to the impulse that flows from deep within a stillness of mind and body.

My body may be unmoving, but my mind is far from still. I am acutely aware of others in the room. Some begin to spin and dance, and my mind wonders—judges—how they could possibly be staying connected to the impulse to move and be moving so quickly. I worry that they will think that the woman awkwardly huddled in the corner is too dense to understand the instructions or impossibly slow at connecting with her own stillness. I am tempted to move in a way I think will help stretch out the muscles in my back, but the discomfort in my body and Daphne's constant reminders not to move until the impulse to do so comes from deep within stop me.

Finally, after what feels like an embarrassingly long time but is probably only a few minutes, I lose track of what others are doing, I let go of worrying about what they might be thinking about me. I decide that if I do not move during this whole exercise it does not matter, and I begin to relax into my spot on the floor, into my body and my breath. And I become still. Slowly I feel an impulse to stretch out one leg, not as a decision but as a kind of flow that comes from the stillness at the center of my body, like a spring bubbling up through the earth. Slowly I move my leg. And again I am still. And the flow moves my other leg out in front of me as I gently slide to the floor and roll onto my belly.

I am unaware of time, but later Daphne tells us that the exercise lasted about twenty minutes. For most of that time I move slowly, staying close to the floor, rolling and stretching and stopping, always keeping most of my attention on the still center. When Daphne asks us to gradually come to our feet and join her in the middle of the room I find, miraculously, that my back, shoulders, and neck are free of all pain. The spasm has gone, the knots have loosened, my shoulder blades are once again mobile. I can hardly believe it. Given a chance, my body, guided by a deep stillness I could become aware of only when I stopped fighting what was, has found the physical movements and positions that have released my tense muscles. I had not been trying to release the pain in my body. I had simply been present and aware and followed the immediate impulse to move or be still.

This is what not-doing is like: movement that comes from a deep and centered experience of simply being here and now; movement that is not preoccupied with or attached to results; movement that focuses on the quality of the moment. I have shared this very basic form of contemplative movement with men and women who have come to workshops I have facilitated and watched the struggle that mirrors my own on many of their faces. Some do not wait at all but begin to follow familiar learned movements of yoga or dance or tai chi. Others wait with increasing anxiety, afraid that the impulse to move will simply never come and they will be left sitting or standing alone while everyone else is engaged in some wonderful dance from which they have been excluded.

We do not trust what we are, an echo of the Beloved whom we secretly fear searches for everyone except us. If it is difficult to trust the deep stillness at our core to guide us in a simple movement exercise, how much harder will it be to trust that we can find and listen to what arises from that quiet center in the midst of our daily lives, where the cultural imperative to do, the push to move unceasingly according to what we or others think is appropriate and necessary, is continually being shouted within and around us? Even if we like the idea of a still and dynamic presence within and around all that is, we may doubt our own ability to become aware of this deep stillness. So we avoid opportunities to stop, afraid that we will be uniquely deficient, unable to hear the call.

Coming home from the wilderness after the first seven days of my quest, I decide to maintain my intent to be in ceremony for forty days. I remain in the familiar setting of my home, surrounded by the concerns and distractions of everyday life but committed to finding a different way of being with them, wanting to try easier. The last thirty-three days of this time of retreat are not as physically challenging as the first seven, but they offer me a progressively clearer answer to my question about how to live connected both to all of what I know myself to be and to that which is larger than myself. With no work commitments during this time, I allow myself to follow the flow of my days, much the way I would have at the wilderness site, taking my time with my practices of prayer, meditation, and yoga, eating and sleeping when I feel the impulse, and taking care of my home. Although my sons are around and some close friends know I have returned, most people expect me to be out of contact for forty days, and I do not get in touch with them. I have made no agreements or promises for this time, have few obligations or commitments to fulfill. And so each day I am able to sit still, able to connect with an awareness of the essence of what I am and then to experiment, walking through my day with one level of attention perpetually on this awareness, watching to see if and when I lose consciousness of this still center, observing when I get caught up in the drivenness to get even this right.

I follow my intuitive nose. One morning I find myself singing a chant to the female Buddha, Tara: *Om Tara Tu Tare Ture Svaha*. After an hour of chanting I rise and follow the impulse to wander around the city on foot. As I walk the downtown streets for the rest of the day I continue to chant, quietly under my breath or silently to myself. The city looks different: human, connected, beautiful in both the splendor and squalor of life continuing. Despite the fact that I walk through areas of the city considered less safe than others, I feel very safe. Being fully present, I know I am able to assess the ever-changing circumstances around me and respond in the moment if necessary.

The taste of not-doing is very different from the taste of doing. After the first two weeks of recuperating from my time in the wilderness, I begin to participate in household tasks when the impulse to do so arises within me. But I discover that the moment I move away from simply following the impulse to rake up leaves in the yard to getting-the-whole-yard-cleaned-up-before-it-gets-dark, I lose awareness of the spaciousness at the center of simply being. The minute I am focused on and attached to a goal to be achieved in the future, I am no longer fully present, no longer open to stopping if and when the impulse to do so comes. I lose touch with the joy in the task, with the sense of being in the flow of the day, and I become tired and irritated with those around me. This is falling asleep. Walking asleep, moving in the world disconnected from our essential core, can be dangerous; it means our choices are based not on an accurate picture of what is but on what we want or fear is true. At best, actions based on an inaccurate picture of what is are unlikely to succeed in creating the change we desire. At worst, they will create greater suffering.

There are a thousand ways to go to sleep, to walk through our lives unaware of and unable to be with what is and so unconscious of what and who we are. Beyond the obvious choices to move away from what is by using a variety of substances—food, alcohol, nicotine, drugs, caffeine—the culturally preferred way of making sure we don't wake up is to keep ourselves perpetually exhausted with constant activity, endless work, and the consumption of overwhelming amounts of information: to *do* continually. And even when some of us reject the quest for more material wealth or social status, we do not necessarily break the pattern but turn instead to the pursuit of spiritual development. Either way, we are in constant motion internally or externally. We are rarely still. We seldom find silence. We do not rest. And tired people do not want to wake up, don't have the energy to wake up, can't even fathom it as a possibility.

We will never be deeply happy or truly able to live and love fully until we find our way of living from an awareness of the deep stillness at the center of what we are. It is not so much that what we are at the deepest level wants to wake up, to be aware, to love, to create peace and truth and beauty, but that our essential nature *is* wakefulness, awareness, love, peace, truth, and beauty. To hear the call we only need to listen. But sometimes we can listen only when our illusions of control and safety have been shattered, when we are lying on the ground—figuratively or literally in the wilderness—weeping and ready to say, as Rumi wrote:

I didn't come here of my own accord.
Whoever brought me here will have to come and take me home.

Meditation on Contemplative Movement

Stand or sit in the middle of an open space, preferably a room or area where you will not be interrupted or observed. Make sure you are wearing comfortable clothing that will not inhibit movement. Remove your shoes and socks if you are comfortable with this. Decide on the length of time you will do this movement meditation, allowing the time (ten to fifteen minutes to start) to act as a container that frees you from repeatedly deciding whether to stop or continue. You may wish to set an alarm clock to avoid looking at the time during the meditation.

Spend a few moments simply settling into your spot. Take three deep breaths, inhaling through your nose and exhaling through your mouth. Allow your shoulders to drop and your weight to come into the bottom half of your body. Be aware of your surroundings, the feel of the floor or ground beneath you, the temperature of the room, the light at this time of day. Be aware of your body, breathing into each body part and becoming aware of the sensations or lack of sensations in each aspect of your body. Breathe into your feet . . . and breathe out from your feet. Breathe into your legs, first one and then the other . . . and out from your legs. Breathe into your pelvis and belly, feeling it expand with the inhale . . . and contract with the exhale. Become aware of your lower back, breathing into the muscles there and exhaling from your lower back. Breathe into your middle back, feeling your rib cage expand and contract with the inhale and exhale. Be aware of your upper back, your neck and shoulders. Now bring your attention to your chest, breathing into

your heart and feeling your lungs expand and contract with each
inhale and exhale, letting go around the heart as the air leaves
your body. Breathe into your hands, your forearms and elbows
. . . your upper arms and up into your collarbone and shoulders
. . . allowing the arms to drop on the exhale. Be aware of your
throat . . . and breathe up into your face . . . around the jaw and
mouth . . . the eyes and cheeks . . . the forehead . . . bones of
the skull . . . becoming aware of the shape and weight of your
head and letting go of any tension or tiredness in your face with
the exhale.

Be aware now of your whole body, standing or sitting where
you are, aware of your physical being from the top of your head to
the tips of your fingers and toes. Breathe into your whole body.
Allow any thoughts that come to slip effortlessly away like pearls
on silk. And now, focusing on the center of your body, open to the
possibility of movement. Do not move unless the impulse to do so
comes from a still deep place within. Give yourself permission not
to move, to stand or sit in this place for the entire time you have
set aside for this meditation. It does not matter if you move or
how far or fast you move. If you feel the impulse to move, follow
it, moving only as fast as you can without losing connection to
that impulse that comes moment to moment from deep within.
Pause if you find yourself unconsciously following a previously
learned movement or you lose your sense of the deep connection
to the impulse to move, remaining still and waiting until it finds
you again. Allow your body to change its position, to move and
come to stillness repeatedly if this is where the impulse to move
takes you.

When the time you have set is up, be still for a few breaths, tasting the difference between movement that is inner directed and action that is attached to and seeks to achieve a specific outcome. Allow yourself to imagine continuing your day connected to a deep sense of inner stillness, allowing all actions to arise from this sense of spaciousness at the center of who you are.

Three

What You Are

*Remember what you are, and let this knowing
take you home to the Beloved with every breath.*

I am lying in my bed, ready to go to sleep, shortly after 11:00 P.M. I am relaxed, quiet, listening. I hear the sound of the streetcar rumble by on its tracks, the whirl of the overhead fan in the hallway, the faint sound of my neighbor playing his piano on the other side of the townhouse wall. I hear my cat snoring gently at the end of my bed, and I feel the cool cotton sheet on my legs, the smooth pillowcase under my cheek. I look into the darkness and see a line of light from the street lamp outside the window at the top of the indigo curtains. Random thoughts float by: Brendan's comment at dinner about the American president George W. Bush's latest announcement concerning the "War on Terror"; Nathan's request that I make him a hair appointment tomorrow. I neither pursue these thoughts nor push them away. They simply float by. Although I am aware of feeling tired, I am not anticipating sleep. I feel my body rising and falling with my breath and the faint reverberations of my heart beating in my chest.

It is a rare moment. I am fully present. I am not doing any-thing. I am just . . . here. And then . . . I am gone. I am not asleep. In fact, I feel more awake than I have ever been. Those things I pri-marily identify as my self most of the time—thoughts of the day, passing sensations of pleasure or discomfort, feelings of tiredness or contentment that come and go—have receded. They are still there but they are distant, like a TV in the corner of the room with the volume turned down to a whisper.

And there is this vastness, this spaciousness that is at once com-pletely empty and overwhelmingly full of aliveness, at once right up against my face and simultaneously behind my eyes, filling me. There are no thoughts, descriptive, reflective, discursive, or other-wise. It is as if a curtain has parted and I am staring down the center of an opening into what I know without thinking always has been and always will be with a consistency and a continuity unknown to the perpetually changing thoughts, events, and items that fill my daily life. There is a sense of participating in a vast holiness both in-side me and surrounding me, but there is no distinguishable inside or outside, it is all me and yet . . . more. I am not filled with stillness and peace. I am stillness and peace, and the notion that I have ever been or will ever be anything else is unthinkable, because there sim-ply is no thinking or feeling or sensing, no past or future. With a kind of wordless clarity I know that I am and always have been and always will be surrounded by, participating in, and an embodiment of this vast and sacred presence that fills my awareness now by virtue of simply being. With a wordless clarity I know that this indescrib-able presence is paradoxically and simultaneously both the essence of what I am and the nature of that which is larger than myself. It is the Great Mystery. It is what I am made of, what everything and everyone is made of. It is what we participate in with every breath.

And without thought, everything—the world, my life—makes sense, is complete in some strange unexplainable way. I am emptied of all that I normally identify as my quest for meaning—the questions and doubts and beliefs and feelings I experience and struggle with each day—and yet simultaneously full, whole, complete. It is overwhelmingly simple and yet totally inexplicable. If someone asked me who I was and why I was here, the answer would be the same, could only be: This! This completeness is both what I am and why I am here.

I don't know how long I stay like this. In this awareness the idea of time has no meaning. There is only a perpetual now. And then at some point, I think, "Holy shit! What was that? I made it! I made it beyond the incessant chatter in my head into just . . . being here, now!" The act of naming my experience and celebrating this "achievement" has, of course, moved me back into a fuller awareness of and at least partial identification with my thoughts and feelings. But the experience of that place within me, the awareness of that spacious and yet full and dynamic stillness that is beyond, behind, and within everything, and the certainty that this is the very nature of inner and outer reality, stays with me. I sit up and flip on the light next to my bed. Everything in the room is as it was, but the room appears to be filled with a strange light, as if the air itself is infused with a fine gold dust. I blink and rub my eyes, but the strange luminosity remains.

This acute awareness of the essence of all that is ebbs and flows with the next day's activities but never totally vanishes. It's as if the two halves of the curtain of unconsciousness can never come completely back together again once they have been parted, and so a gap—sometimes a slim crack and at other times a wide opening—remains through which the awareness of what is can shine.

Writing or talking about an experience that is beyond thought and so beyond words can be problematic. The temptation is to invent a new word to capture the experience, but that new word would hold little meaning for anyone but me. I play with capitalizing simple words, like *Being* or *Presence,* to describe the indescribable. But these become vague terms and create the illusion that what is embedded in every ordinary moment of existence is somehow special and removed from the everyday. Relegating the sacred to that which is special—to moments, people, activities, or things we see as separate and exceptional—is part of what has allowed us to stop caring for all aspects of the world, is how we have lost track of what we are and the meaning embedded in every moment of our lives.

So I content myself with using phrases that point toward the taste and touch and feel of the direct experience of what we are, knowing these words are only an approximation, a pointing toward that which can be experienced but can never be captured with concepts or words. An ancient Buddhist story tells us that the teachings—the words—are like a finger pointing to the moon and warns us not to mistake them for the moon itself. Remember that what I am pointing to with phrases such as *a deep and dynamic stillness at the center, a vast and all-inclusive spaciousness,* or *a silent and certain wholeness* is not confined to or defined by these words. These words, my stories, are only a way of pointing to what can be experienced but cannot be named. They are, as Rumi wrote, *the smoke the fire gives off.* They are not the fire itself. When I write about my experience of this fire that is my essential nature as also that which surrounds and reaches for and calls to me, I have capitalized the name I give to it, calling it God or Beloved or the Sacred Mystery. In truth there is no separation. There is only the one fire running through the center of all that is.

I have experienced the acute sense of my essential stillness many times in my life, often for only a moment. It's as if the normal activity of life, the noise and doing around and within me, suddenly has a crack in it, and I find myself unexpectedly and overwhelmingly at peace in the gap between this exhale and the next inhale. Sometimes this happens in a more sustainable way when doing a meditation practice, and often it comes spontaneously when I am in the beauty of the wilderness I love. Out on the vision quest I was able to spend long hours just being with the natural world around me, and I became aware of a vast silence that is at the center of all sound. In a world of too much noise, both inner and outer, the very cells of my being ache to drink in this silence, to taste this stillness. I wrote in my journal on the second day of my quest:

> *Here in this place I touch a silence so complete*
> *it makes my ears ache and my heart startle in confusion.*
> *After all these years of sound,*
> *after all the noise that has come between me and being fully alive,*
> *it swallows me whole,*
> *this great silence*
> *that comes in the moment after the wind dies*

and the pines suddenly hold still.
It takes me by surprise,
this unexpected quiet
after the red squirrel runs over the log
and up the tree and across the branch,
disappearing into the deep woods.
It comes as the sun slides down the sky and all is quiet,
the songbirds holding their breath for a moment
as if by common agreement,
the night peepers not yet singing.
And for a moment lying here in the fading light
on a sun-warmed bed of pine needles
even the sound of my own heartbeat
—a thrumming deep inside—
is gone.
And all there is, is the great silence that holds it all.
And something inside lets go,
and I rest in the arms of the Beloved.

This is the home we all long for, the belonging at the center of the ache we feel for something more, even when our lives are going well. It is a longing to know, to experience, both our own wholeness and the presence of that which can hold that wholeness, that which is larger than ourselves. The two are inextricably linked. An experience of one always includes an opening to the other. We are given, in this experience of our essence, knowledge of both who we are and why we are here. When we move into simply being, we touch the meaning we need in order to live fully.

To hear and answer the call to commit fully to being in my life, I must learn to be with whatever is, even when that is a lack of conscious awareness of the still center. If I am exclusively caught in my identity with daily concerns and passing thoughts and feelings, I mistake constantly changing circumstances for all there is, and my sense of well-being gets batted about like a Ping-Pong ball depending upon moment-to-moment conditions within and around me, conditions that are largely beyond my control. Without the perspective of knowing my essence, I will suffer, and in doing so I cannot help but spread suffering in the world.

I am unloading the week's groceries from my car. I am in a good mood, calm, feeling like I am on top of the tasks of the day. As I return to my car for another load a young neighbor, a boy of thirteen, drops his bicycle in front of my door and turns to leave. My townhouse door faces the communal storage shed where bicycles are supposed to be kept.

I am immediately on alert. I have spoken to him about this before. "Hold it, fella," I say, trying to sound friendly but firm. "That's not where the bike belongs. Put it in the shed."

He does not stop walking past my car, away from the bike. "Can't," he says monosyllabically. "Don't have time. Late for work." I stare in disbelief at his receding back and imagine one of the oranges in my grocery bag hitting him squarely in the back of the head.

"If you leave it there," I say, my voice rising in volume and threat, "I will put it in the middle of the courtyard, and if it gets stolen, tough!"

He hesitates for a moment and looks over his shoulder at me, shrugs, and then says in that dismissive tone that only thirteen-year-old boys can really master, "Whatever," and keeps on walking away.

I am livid. In less than ten seconds I have gone from being calm and relaxed to feeling tense and ready to pounce. I have moved from feeling that all is right with the world to wanting to do some damage to a fellow human being. Even as it happens, some small part of my consciousness is aware of how fast and complete the change has been, and I wonder. But this is no time for introspection. Fuming, I move the bike so I can gain access to my door and half drag, half toss the thing into the center of the courtyard. Continuing to unload my car, I rail internally about the inconsiderateness of people generally and young males in particular.

My son Nathan arrives home, entering the far end of the courtyard just in time to see me move the bike. As he helps me unload the rest of the groceries I tell him what has happened. He listens quietly and smiles, no doubt relieved not to be the one on the receiving end of my self-righteous anger. "So," he says slowly as we finish our task and stand in the kitchen, "what are you going to do if the bike is stolen? I mean, next thing you know he'll be out in the parking lot keying your car. Then what are you going to do, grab his little brother and beat him up?"

I pause. I can see his point. I don't want to see his point, but it's hard to miss living in a world where current conflicts are threatening to spiral out of control and endanger us all. If I can't turn away from doing something in retribution to another when the offense is as small as an inconsiderately placed bicycle, what hope is there for one nation to turn aside from venting outrage in violence when serious harm has been suffered? I go outside and move the bike into the shed so it will be neither stolen nor in my way.

Coming back into my house, I am still fuming. I pause in the middle of the kitchen and consider what I can do. Some minute corner of consciousness remains and asks, "What is this really about?" I know I can sit with the feelings and find out what is behind this rage. I don't want to sit with it. I want to be right. Because I am right! But I can see how clinging to being right, this wanting the situation to be different than it is—wanting the boy to admit I am right, apologize for his actions, and put his bike in the shed—is causing me to suffer and has almost caused me to create more suffering in my community.

So I sit. I breathe. I do not move away from the feelings of rage pulsing through me. I am simply with them fully. It doesn't take very long, a couple of minutes really, and there it is, behind all the anger: a feeling of deep weariness, of being worn out by all the normal caregiving involved in raising two sons. And below this tiredness there is the fear—the terror—that although my sons are grown there will be adolescent males finding me, seeking me out wherever I go for the rest of my life, demanding that I pick up after them. I laugh, and the anger is released. What this is about is taking care of myself, allowing myself to rest, feeding my own tired body and soul. Seeing this, I suddenly hear the young boy's "whatever" not so much as defiance and inconsiderateness but as his own weariness. He, like most thirteen-year-olds, simply does not want or need another mother telling him what to do.

Learning to simply be with what is and so finding the still center, if only for a moment, shifts things, lets us be with our feelings instead of being unconsciously led around by them. With the perspective offered by deep stillness, I can see the big picture. I may still experience discomfort and sometimes pain, but when I do it does not feel life-threateningly unbearable.

Years ago, I read an interview with the Dalai Lama. The interviewer was surprised to hear the Dalai Lama say that he regretted that he had not been present at his brother's death. The interviewer, assuming probably correctly that the Dalai Lama has a pretty continuous sense of an infinite presence within and around him, assumed incorrectly that this awareness of the essential nature of all reality would shield him from any pain caused by being a human being who loves not just humanity but particular humans. The Dalai Lama is a human being, and a human being is a wholeness that is both this essence and an individual self with a history and passing thoughts and feelings—an ego. When we know our wholeness, when we are consciously aware of both ego and essence, we feel the pain of loss in our lives not as crippling devastation that makes us want to give up on life itself, but as human sadness that we know will change with time, as all feelings do. The Dalai Lama had not been crippled with guilt or agony over the circumstances of his brother's death, but he could acknowledge and be with his sense of loss, his sadness that he had not been able to be with his brother to offer whatever help he could in his passing. Awareness of the essence of what we are does not take us away from our feelings, but it can give us a perspective that makes it easier to be with these feelings

without identifying exclusively with, suffering painfully over, or acting upon them.

When I stopped doing and could simply be with what was for
just a few moments, I experienced a commonality between myself
and the thirteen-year-old neighbor my mind was making the
Enemy. Awareness of the essence of what we are, of what all things
are, shows us the interbeingness of reality.

Meditating on the interbeingness of reality in the morning, I
become aware of the constant interdependence of all life. As I
drive my car on the freeway later that day I realize that my physical safety is at least as dependent upon the skill, care, and attention of the drivers around me as upon my own abilities. Then I
become aware of all the factors beyond my control upon which
my physical well-being relies: the skill of those who designed,
built, and inspected the vehicle I am driving; the competence of
those who constructed the road I am on; the labor of those who
grew and picked and packaged the food I prepared and ate this
morning . . . and the illusion of independence and control dis-
solves. I can see how my physical, mental, and emotional well-
being, and the well-being of those I love, is linked in a thousand
ways to the lives and choices of many others. Living in a global
community has made this interdependence easier to see, and yet
we often still insist on pursuing a self-destructive individual and
collective exclusivity, an attitude that posits *my* own or *my* country's or *my* family's peace and prosperity as separate from or more
important than the well-being of all beings—human and non-
human—on this planet.

A few years ago I went to stay at a remote cabin deep within the Canadian wilderness not far from the area where I had grown up. I went out alone and paddled a canoe along a shoreline that was not accessible by road. Pulling my canoe up on shore, I started to walk through the dense bush, climbing the steep rocky shore until I found a high open area where the ground was covered with blueberry bushes. I settled down in the warmth of the late summer sun to eat some berries and watch the wind move over the dark blue water of the lake below. As I picked the berries I noticed something small and white on the ground beneath one of the bushes and, gently pushing back the plants, discovered the delicate skull of a small bird. The flesh had decayed, adding its form and releasing its energy into the soil where the bushes sent out their roots. As I chewed on the sweet fruit I could feel how everything was connected: how the body of this small bird had returned to the earth, nourishing the plant that grew the berries I was taking into my body; how the food I was eating was being used by my body to stay healthy and balanced, releasing some of the energy from its biological processes in the warm moisture of my breath; how this moisture was being absorbed by the wind that was slowly forming clouds overhead that would release life-sustaining moisture, including the small bit from my body, to the earth in a different place. I lay my body down on the ground and acknowledged in a new way that my flesh would one day return to the soil and, like the body of that small bird, be absorbed back into the growing processes of other plants and animals.

Awareness of your essence, that spacious wholeness at the center of all that is, changes interbeingness from an idea, from a description of temporary or particular conditions, to consciousness of the very nature of reality itself. When you experience your own deep and dynamic stillness, you become conscious that all things are made of the same sacred presence, that all things emanate from and return to and are never separated from a vast and sacred wholeness. Knowing this, how can my prayers—or my heart—exclude anyone or anything?

As I walk through the remainder of the forty days of ceremony in the comfort of my own home, I find that as important as essence-awareness is to my sense of perspective and wholeness, I can't make it happen. I can return to those places and practices that in the past have corresponded with instances of experiencing this infinite stillness. I can be willing to experience and be available to this awareness, but I cannot with my will make it happen. In part this is because doing is not what is required. Not-doing—a willingness to get out of my own way, to stop following every thought, feeling, or sensation into doing, to stop resisting and surrender to what is—is what is required.

This is harder than it sounds. The ego, my identity with passing thoughts, feelings, and sensations, wants to be in charge of the process and consequences of gaining essence-awareness. We want God on our own terms. But the reality is that we cannot *do* anything to bring this experience to us, nor can we control how it will transform our perspective or what it will require when it comes to the willing heart. When we consciously stop fighting, consciously stop trying to change or ignore what is, we become available to experiencing what we are. And in the moment when we move into that great silence and taste the stillness and joy we are, we shake our heads, not knowing whether to laugh or cry as we see our resistance to what is as the silliest and saddest way to spend our lives, the most futile waste of our precious time together, as the painfully obvious cause of all the suffering in our hearts and the world.

It is tempting to regard the essence of what we are, that vast still center that does not change and gives us a perspective that allows us to be more easily compassionate and present, as somehow more real than the ever-changing patterns of thoughts, feelings, and sensations we call the ego. Many spiritual traditions designate the ego as merely a vehicle, at best a means, for the self-realization of essence. Others consider it an illusion or a kind of slipcover for the soul, to be discarded when no longer needed. But temporary or changing does not mean unreal. What you see depends on your perspective. Heisenberg showed that light would appear to behave as either a particle or a wave, depending upon how the observer set up the experiment, how she or he chose to look at light. When I look at another or myself one way I see an ego: a differentiated, individuated set of particular and changing thoughts, feelings, and sensations. When I look at another or myself in a different way I see essence: that vast, silent, unchanging presence that is always there. Two ways of seeing one whole human being. The call I hear asks me to expand, to learn a third way, a way of seeing and recognizing the wholeness that is greater than the sum of the parts, that excludes neither ego nor essence, if I am to live the meaning of a human life fully awake.

Ironically, wanting to live exclusively from an awareness of our essential nature can come only from exclusive or heavily weighted identification with our ego. Essence—mine, yours, that of the mystery from which we come—can hold it all, asserts no concept of right or wrong, has no attachment to doing it perfectly. These are the ego's judgments and goals, and even these are held with compassion by the deep and sacred stillness we are. When I have been aware primarily of my essence, when I found my thoughts and feelings suddenly in the background and this overwhelming sense of simply being at the center of my consciousness, what I was in that moment excluded nothing, looked upon all forms, including my own personal ambitions and fears and struggles, with deep compassion. This spaciousness that is what we are is not indifferent to the suffering we feel when we have forgotten what we are. It reaches out to us, calls to us. And it does this even when we have no notion of anything beyond or behind our small daily concerns, no conscious experience of what we are or why we are here, showing us our innocence—our inner essence—calling us to wake up to what we are.

In the summer of 2000, alone at a cabin in the wilderness after a week's vacation with friends and family who have returned to the city, I walk into the forest and discover a small waterfall. There where the stream cascades over well-worn rocks, the trees grow close to each other, allowing only a few thin shafts of sunlight to pierce the dark green canopy above me. The rocks beside the running water are covered with emerald moss. It's like breathing underwater. I sit in this earth-made womb and pray for my life and for my people. Sometimes with prayer you have to take your time, you have to sit and wait for the deepest ache to rise from within and find your lips, wait for the answering call to find you in its own way. The sound of the water rushing over rock, the softness of the moss, the dark cool stillness of this spot where I am sheltered, makes it easy to pray and wait and pray and wait again. And as I sit there for the next few hours, moving through prayers about my daily concerns into my longing to know how best to contribute to the world, I see an image of myself moving through different stages of my life: as a child raising money to pay for schoolbooks for children in India by organizing bake sales; choosing to go into journalism courses at nineteen in the hopes of making a difference in the world by telling true stories; working as a young woman in the social justice movement and later as a social worker wanting to help create change in the world; learning and sharing the teachings of the tribal elders in the hopes of offering guidance and relief to those who are seeking direction in their lives.

For the first time I see how all of what I have done has been motivated at least in part by my desire to alleviate suffering in the world. Instead of the usual feeling of not having done enough, I am overwhelmed with the knowledge of how consistently this thread, this innocence, has run through my life, surviving and becoming mixed with and sometimes shaped by personal needs, unconscious ambitions, erroneous assumptions, and at times ineffective or unconscious actions. I have not been a saint. I have been a human being. And for most of my life I have been a human being with only intermittent consciousness of that still center within myself. Yet somehow what I am, the stuff of which all things are made—that vast and compassionate spaciousness that can hold it all—has been there in the seed of my continuous desire to alleviate suffering in the world.

Sometimes it's important to see your own goodness. That day in the forest I prayed for a way to deepen my daily practice and made a promise to do, every day for the next one thousand days, the ceremony of twenty-two prayers I had been doing periodically for fifteen years. These prayers come from an intertribal shamanic tradition. They name the different manifestations of the Sacred Mystery within and around me, bringing to my awareness the interdependent elements of the seen and unseen worlds. They bring me to stillness and offer me a way to come into conscious alignment with all that is within and around me.

The surprising thing is how easy it has been to do these prayers daily, how effortlessly I have gone every day to my time of contemplative prayer. The one thousand days will be over in June of 2003, but I cannot imagine not continuing. Daily contemplative prayer has become a part of my life. I cannot help but think that the vision I had on that day, the view I was offered of the thread of my consistent desire to alleviate suffering in the world, has been critical in finding this ease. Seeing our innocence, knowing our inherent goodness, we find ourselves worthy of sending out a voice, of putting aside a time of stillness every day to connect to what we are and why we are here.

Our innocence is a reminder of what we are. How you have lived the essence of what we are will be different from how I have lived it. You may see it in the consistent thread of desire in your choices to add beauty to the world through art or science, to be kind, to include those who are at times excluded, to work for justice or fairness, to lighten hearts with humor, to care for family or friends. There are a thousand ways our essential nature can be expressed in the world, infinite ways to hold and love the world. If you look at your life from within that sense of the quiet stillness you are, you will see this inner essence, this innocence, like a bright thread woven throughout the center of your life. It has always been there because it is what you are, and living it consciously is why you are here.

Meditation on Innocence

Sit in a comfortable position, preferably upright but relaxed. Take three deep breaths into your belly, allowing your body to expand with the inhale and contract and drop on the exhale. Send your breath on each inhale into all parts of your body—feet and legs, hands and arms, neck and head—and allow all stress or tension or tiredness to leave as you exhale. Breathing normally, gently bring your focus to your breath, allowing all other thoughts or sensations to simply drift by as they come, neither resisting nor engaging them with your attention. Let the breath be at the center of your stillness.

Into this place of deep stillness, allow an image of yourself to come, remembering a time when you offered something to someone else. Let it be something as small as holding a door open for an elderly person or extending comfort to a child who had skinned his or her knee. It may have been a moment when you shared something of yourself, telling a story of your life with another. It may have been a moment when you created beauty for another in how you listened or how you offered something—a meal, a smile, an encouraging word. It may have been a moment when you turned away from seeking retribution. Allow whatever comes to be there without judgment about what you think the impact of what you offered was, without analyzing to what degree your desire to offer something was mixed with other motives.

Sit with this image, and feel within it the thread of your genuine desire to offer something to the world, to another. Perhaps you wanted to ease another's pain or to create intimacy or offer support. Perhaps you wanted to add beauty to the moment with humor or insight or compassion. Let the thread of your own innocence, your own desire to alleviate suffering and contribute to the world something of meaning, reveal itself to you.

Be with this sense of your own innocence, and let it lead you to other instances in your life when you have acted out of the desire to create beauty or offer solace. See the different ways this thread of innocence has been woven with a thousand others in your choices. Let instances from when you were a child come to you. Let the reality of your own goodness reveal itself to you. Be with it and the feelings it raises without judgment. If you begin to analyze the instances that come to mind, simply bring your attention back to your breath, letting your mind clear, and wait for a new image. See and know your own goodness.

Four

Who You Are

Hold tenderly who you are, and let a deeper knowing
color the shape of your humanness.

At some point during my forty-day retreat I realized that the way I was spending these days—cultivating my awareness of my still center and allowing all movement to flow from this awareness, practicing not-doing—is the way I need to live. But I know that my ego's fiery temperament and my natural propensity to focus on achievement often make this difficult. That's why I'd gone out on the vision quest in the first place. Although I had not said it explicitly, I wanted an ego transplant, wanted my driven, judgmental self surgically or spiritually removed.

Before I went off into the wilderness to try to ditch my troublesome ego, I'd been faking self-acceptance for years.

I am watching a videotape of an interview I did for TV Ontario. The interviewer, Paula Todd, is engaging and sincere. I do not generally like watching myself on TV. I can see too many things I would do or say differently if I had the chance, but this interview seems to be going pretty well. Paula asks me about the physical abuse in my first marriage and about being raped when I was a young woman. I am not uncomfortable talking about these difficult times in my life. These are stories of my life, they are not who I am. Paula questions how a bright young woman like me could have made the poor choices that were at least partly responsible for creating situations that resulted in or temporarily perpetuated suffering for myself. This is a question I have asked myself many times, and I share what I know about by own propensity for thinking I am rescuing others and my denial of intuitive warning signals, tendencies that can often get us into dangerous situations. I tell her about the healing that occurred for me when I attended a martial arts course in the Mojave Desert many years after I was raped.

At the end of an intensive two-week course the women who had been trained were tested by being attacked three times one-on-one by men committed to helping women empower themselves to walk safely in the world. The men wore protective gear, the women did not. We were told that the attacks would be no-holds-barred and would continue until the instructor, Dawn, a petite woman who worked as a bodyguard in Los Angeles, called out, "Cut!" We had to deliver one or two blows to the man attacking us that would have incapacitated him long enough for us to get away if he had not been wearing protective gear.

As we began, the women who wanted to be tested stood along the edge of a large matted area. One at a time the men wandered around within the circle watching the women and seeking to attack someone when she least expected it. Shortly after we began, one of the women broke her leg struggling with a man who'd grabbed her. We all heard it snap beneath her as she went down heavily. It shook us, but most of us stayed to be tested. Many of us had been raped or beaten. We needed to know we could defend ourselves.

The first time I was attacked I made a slow but steady response, finally delivering a blow to the man's protected eyes that would have given me time to get away if this had been a real attack. But the second time, the man who attacked me had been wandering around the circle joking. I was laughing, unprepared, my guard down. When he grabbed me and threw me I arced through the air and landed flat on my back in a way that closely resembled how I had been thrown when I was raped. The man participating in the testing did not know this, but the women in the circle did. Earlier in the week we had reenacted the rape scenes experienced by women in the group, looking for possible ways each woman could have protected herself if she had had the skills and knowledge she was now being given. The man attacking me heard the sharp intake of breath among many of the women around the circle when I hit the ground. He could see I'd had the wind knocked out of me and was badly shaken, but his instructions were to go for it until the instructor told him to stop. So he continued to come at me.

I struggled to fight, but I didn't want to. I felt as if I had landed in a large tub of warm bathwater. Suddenly I didn't care what happened. It felt like it just didn't matter. I heard Dawn calling to me as if from very far away. "Don't do that, Oriah!" she yelled. "You've been here before. Don't check out! Fight! Fight for yourself!"

Hearing her voice, I struggled to come out of my lethargy as the man landed on top of me. It was like moving through molasses, but slowly and steadily I began to fight, and finally, after five minutes of constant struggle, I managed to deliver one of the blows we had been taught to incapacitate an attacker. Shaken at how I'd responded to the attack, I hesitated to be tested again, but I put myself back at the edge of the testing area. The third time a man grabbed me I flew into action without hesitation, landing repeated take-out blows almost immediately. Dawn had to yell "Cut!" four times before I heard her.

When I finish telling this story to the TV interviewer, she asks me, "So you would tell a woman who was being attacked to fight?"

I respond calmly but without hesitation, "Absolutely. I would tell her to fight. Fight as if your life depends upon it, because it does."

Watching the interview on tape, I cringe and feel the gap between the self-acceptance I hope and sometimes pretend to have achieved and the desire to be different than I am. I have answered her question without thinking yet my response does not reflect my internal struggle with the question. There is a difference between using whatever minimum level of force is necessary to stop violence that is happening in the moment and dropping bombs on those we suspect might do us harm in the future. But I also know it can be a slippery slope from one to the other, and watching the world I begin to suspect that any violence against another, even when it is justified as self-defense, will ultimately only ever lead to more violence. But still, when asked, I have responded with a gut-level certainty I suspect would determine my immediate actions if I or someone else were being physically harmed. At the very least I want to be someone who, even if she is willing to physically defend herself or others and would advise others to do the same, would do so with an air of regret or hesitation, with less conviction and certainty.

But that's not who I am. Self-acceptance is a practice, a willingness to slowly expand our ability to see ourselves as we are and simply be with what we see. I am a passionate, outspoken woman. I have a tendency to want rules but a mind and heart that simply will not let me settle into one-size-fits-all ethical absolutes. I think fast—which does not always mean clearly—and talk faster. I want to be wisely quiet, mysteriously silent, deeply contemplative. And sometimes I am all of these things. But when I am with the world I am more often directive, opinionated, and passionately expressive. Sometimes this makes me discerning and effective. Occasionally it means I can be downright inspiring. But sometimes it just makes me relentlessly judgmental and annoyingly bossy. I realize that other personalities have their own challenges, but on occasion I have convinced myself that I have been overburdened with a personality that does not make it easy to live a spiritual life.

The truth is, no life is inherently more "spiritual" than another, no personality or set of ego characteristics more readily available to an awareness of the still and sacred presence we are than another. All personalities have slightly different struggles on the road to waking up to who we are and why we are here. Some will have to sit with the urge to strike out when angry while others will have to struggle with their tendency to repress anger and the consequences that brings. Some may have to learn to be quiet more often while others have to learn to speak out. Some may need to act more quickly or more often while others more frequently need to sit still and wait. We all have patterns of behavior and preferences that come from a combination of our inherent temperament and developmental learning, just like we have certain physical characteristics as a result of nature and nurture. Wanting to wake up tomorrow—or at the end of a vision quest—with a different personality, a transformed ego, is a little like hoping I will wake up in the morning five inches taller: a desire that continues my war with reality.

This does not mean we are doomed to unconsciously live out the patterns of our ego. It means that we have to know ourselves, have to bring to consciousness with deep honesty our tendencies and patterns, our strengths and weaknesses, our vulnerabilities and fears, if we are to find real freewill choices in how we live. When I told the TV interviewer that a woman's life depended upon fighting someone who was trying to harm her, I was not merely referring to the chance that she could be physically killed if she did not effectively defend herself. The biggest opponent I faced during that martial arts testing was not the man who was attacking me. My real struggle was with my own feeling that it did not matter if I was harmed, did not matter if I lived or died. On some profound level I had to make the choice we all have to make if we are to respond to the call at the center of our lives: I had to choose to be here, in a human life. Choosing my human life in that moment required that I physically defend myself.

Ego awareness, an individuated sense of self that identifies with patterns of ever-changing thoughts, feelings, sensations, and life situations, is necessary to make this choice. Essence awareness, the consciousness of the eternal inherent being we are, is not particularly concerned with the details of the life I am living, knows that all thoughts, feelings, and situations will pass and that what is eternal and infinite within us will remain. But essence awareness alone does not make a human life. A human life is lived in our very particular and real daily choices. Essence awareness can give us the perspective needed to ensure we do not drown in the minutiae of daily living or become so exclusively identified with our egos that the constantly changing reality and others' ego agendas feel life threatening. But ego awareness is also needed if we are to inhabit fully the life we have, if we are to make conscious daily choices about what we do, where we go, and how we live. Lack of attachment to having things work out the way we want them to is not the same thing as the indifference that comes from not fully committing to a human life. When I was lying on that mat during the martial arts test feeling like it did not matter whether or not I fought to protect myself, I was not connecting to the lack of attachment to outcome that can come when I am aware of my essential nature. I was, in that moment and more generally at that time in my life, unable to cherish and occupy fully my human life.

Life without essence awareness lacks meaning and connection. Life without ego awareness lacks fire and direction.

Language is limited. It separates what is inseparable. Writing, I refer to our egos as who we are and our essence as what we are. But the reality, as psychiatrist and writer Mark Epstein points out, is that we don't have parts. We are whole human beings. Separating our ideas of ego and essence tempts us into trying to leave behind what we see as problematic—the ego with its ever-changing thoughts and feelings, vulnerable to fear and so to forgetting that being human is more than this. It's not that certain aspects of my ego are more suited than others to living simultaneously with essence awareness. The infinite Mystery that is both the essence of what we are and that which is larger than ourselves excludes nothing. Every characteristic of my ego can be used to open to a deeper awareness of my essence, can facilitate living what and who I am fully. This means that I need to know myself and include in my self-consciousness those aspects of ego I have considered less "spiritual," those aspects I may have tried to bury or ignore or leave behind.

Canadian poet Susan Goyette talks about what is lost when we try to leave behind aspects of ourselves in this poem from her book *The True Names of Birds*.

The True Names of Birds

There are more ways to abandon a child
than to leave them at the mouth of the woods.
Sometimes by the time you find them, they've made up names
for all the birds and constellations, and they've broken
their reflections in the lake with sticks.

With my daughter came promises and vows
that unfolded through time like a roadmap and led me
to myself as a child, filled with wonder for my father
who could make sound from a wide blade of grass

and his breath. Here in the stillness of the forest,
the sun columning before me temple-ancient,
the wonder is what I regret losing most; that wonder
and the true names of birds.

—Susan Goyette

Sometimes we encounter feelings or beliefs that do not fit with who we want to be, aspects of our ego we did not even know we had tried to leave behind. And when we find them again we also find the gifts they brought us, the *wonder* or *the true names of birds* we had forgotten.

It is September 9, 2001, my forty-seventh birthday. Jeff, the man I love and have been with for the past two years, a man I met when I was only fifteen and he was seventeen, gives me a diamond ring. Kissing him, I put it on my finger and move my hand under the reading lamp beside me to watch the light bounce off the facets of the stone, grinning ear to ear. Nathan, my younger son, watches bewildered and amused.

"I don't get it," he says. "You've never really been into diamonds or jewelry or stuff like that, but you are thrilled with this. Why?"

He's right. I have never been particularly interested in gems or jewelry. I did not have a diamond ring when I married his father twenty years ago or when I married my first husband years earlier. I hadn't wanted one. I know about the diamond industry's profit-driven efforts to get us to pay outrageous prices for small clear stones; I understand how marriage and its symbols have often been used by patriarchal institutions to keep women in a position of dependency and less power. Pausing now and considering all this, I take a breath and draw on all my years of deep introspection and spiritual reflection to answer Nathan's question. Holding my left hand to my chest and covering the ring on my finger protectively with my other hand, I say with a certain fierceness that dares him to argue, "I don't know. It's a girl thing. Don't bug me!"

Laughing, I suddenly know it's true. It is a girl thing, a sixteen-year-old girl thing, and it's tied to a feeling I tried to leave behind because it did not seem to fit with who I often am: someone who sees the material world and possessions as less important than the spiritual aspects of life; someone who has maintained and asserted her independence at every opportunity. But beneath these notions of who I am—notions that are not false but only incomplete and changing—I find another longing, a desire to make a choice to be fully in a human life in part by daring to make a 'til-death-do-us-part commitment to another despite my intimate knowledge of how many marriages do not last a lifetime. Symbols gain their power from shared meaning. A diamond in my time and culture is one of many symbols that represents this nonrational and courageous desire to commit to, to be fully "engaged" with love and life. Accepting the ring, I bring to consciousness and accept an aspect of myself that continues to hope and commit and choose life fully despite the blows it has received, despite the inner and outer voices that warn that such dreams are unrealistic in a changing world, voices that seek protection from possible future disappointment.

Is this aspect ego or essence? Neither and both. It is human. Essence is committed to life, is life living itself within us and around us, and ego makes this commitment particular to the life you have. For me, living my commitment to life has included the choice to accept a ring and the invitation to marry and create a home and life with another. For someone else it may entail a different choice.

But whatever the particular choice, hearing and responding to the call to commit fully to a human life can take courage. It can split you open, especially if you have turned away from hearing it for many years, have forgotten the name of that ache in the center of your chest. When we were young our innocence—and to some degree our ignorance—made us brave. Hearing the call, many of us set out to begin a holy pilgrimage, to make a sacred quest of our lives, to risk the unknown. We wanted to take vows to another, to God, to Truth or Beauty or Justice, or to simply being all that we knew or imagined ourselves to be. Later, after we have seen what the world can do—what we can do—it becomes harder, it requires more courage to listen and respond. We try to convince ourselves that we have no time to listen, afraid that the voice no longer calls our name, and when once again we hear the call we grieve for all the vows we have broken. And then we make simpler promises: to listen; to do the best we can today to live a human life awake.

When we first wake up and become conscious of our ego patterns and essential nature we oscillate back and forth between identifying primarily with sometimes newly uncovered thoughts and feelings and experiencing the deep stillness at the center of who we are. Tired of this alternating and wanting to believe that the essential stillness that makes it easier to be compassionate with myself and others is more real than my ego, I went out on a quest asking to be shown how to live exclusively from this consciousness of what I am. But what I found—what I was called to do—was to allow the sacred marriage of ego and essence within myself. I was called to let my essence color the choices my ego makes, to allow the way I act upon the thoughts and feelings and sensations passing through me to be held and guided by an awareness of the sacred stillness at the center of what I am and the presence of that which is larger than myself. I was also called to allow my ego to shape the way I live the essential commitment to life that is what I am, to let the infinite spaciousness at the center of simply being take on the shape of a human woman who loves slow mornings and fast dancing, a human woman who speaks with conviction but often has doubts, a human woman who struggles to find rest and aches to make a difference in the world. I was called to stop the war with my humanness.

Without this marriage of ego and essence, we will tend to identify exclusively with one or the other. In a culture that values individuality and glorifies the immediate satisfaction of personal desires, if only to keep us buying what we cannot afford and do not need, we are more likely to identify exclusively with our ego. If we have had even a momentary experience of our essence—of that expansive being we are—but identify primarily with our ego we will find ourselves suffering from a kind of terminal uniqueness. We become either dangerously inflated, believing that we are God creating and controlling all aspects of reality with our thoughts, or defeated and deflated, feeling we are the worst person alive, failing as no other has to live the essence we have occasionally touched. To let go of exclusively identifying with our ego, we have to give up being the worst or the best.

By contrast, if we want to identify exclusively with our essential nature, we risk denying the ego and cutting ourselves off from its particular wisdom and tying ourselves into knots of denial and delusion about real human needs and frailties. A friend of mine recently went to Burma to study at a Buddhist monastery. One of the teachers there claimed to be an enlightened master, to be completely free of ego, living exclusively from essence. One day my friend was disturbed to witness this teacher striking a child. When he asked the teacher about it later, the teacher insisted that because he was an enlightened master he could strike the child to correct him, as an act of love and without any personal anger or agenda.

Essence awareness accepts and holds it all. Ego awareness can sometimes be helpful in identifying the bullshit.

How do we find this marriage of ego and essence, this fully human life that is the reason we are here? Trying harder won't work. Doing more won't work. We are called to find ease, called to learn the art of not-doing. *We are called to value the power of presence more than we value the presence of power.* There is only one place and time in which the sacred marriage of our ego and essence can happen, only one place and time in which we can fulfill our purpose to be fully and consciously in a human life: here and now.

Meditation on Essence in Human Form

Sit or lie down in a comfortable position and bring your attention to your breath. Take three deep breaths, allowing the inhale to fill your body completely and letting your body drop down onto the surface that supports you as you exhale.

Bring your attention to your body, breathing into your feet and becoming aware of any sensations or lack of sensations that are there. Imagine the bones and muscles beneath the skin. Be with your feet. Now, breathe into your lower legs, first one and then the other. Be aware of the bones running between your ankle and your knee, of the calf muscle and the skin of the lower legs. Be aware of any sensations in this area, just letting what is be, breathing into first one leg and then the other. Now breathe into your upper legs, the thighs from the knees to the hips, aware of the long strong bone at the center of your upper leg, of the muscle and skin, the nerve endings and blood vessels in this part of your body. Fill your thighs with breath, being aware of any sensations in this area, and letting it be the way it is. Now breathe into your hips and pelvis, becoming aware of the bone and the organs of the lower abdomen, the genitals, and buttocks. Be aware of any sensations or lack of sensations, letting them be.

Take a few breaths, aware of your lower body—the hips and pelvis, thighs and knees, the lower legs and ankles and feet—breathing into this area of your body and observing any thoughts or sensations that come and letting them go.

Breathe now into your lower back, into the muscles and bones at the base of your spine. Move your breath and your attention up your back, into the middle of the back where the rib cage and shoulder blades are, feeling them expand and contract with your breath. Be aware of your shoulders, and let your attention and your breath flow down into your arms—the upper arms, elbows, lower arms and hands and fingers, observing any sensations in these areas. Breathe into the front of your torso, letting the belly rise with the inhale and sink with the exhale. Breathe into your heart, filling your lungs and letting your chest expand. Be aware of both your upper body and your hips and legs, sending your breath down throughout this area.

Now bring your attention to your neck and throat, feeling the air move in and out of this area. Breathe into your face, up into the jaw and mouth, feeling your lips and tongue and teeth, aware of any sensations in your cheeks and up into the area around your eyes and nose. Be aware of the sides of your head, of your ears. Breathe into your head, feeling the bones and skin of the skull, aware of any sensations in your face or neck or head.

Breathe into your whole body, aware of your physicality and any sensations that are in the body, and just letting those sensations go. And now . . . with each breath . . . be aware of the energy that makes this body alive. With each breath feel the continual animation of this body, the life force energy that runs through your breath, your blood, your nerve endings, through every cell and molecule and subatomic particle of your body. What makes you alive? What animates this particular form of organic material, organizing it into what we know to be a human being? Feel this force in all parts of yourself, from the tips of your fingers and toes to the top of your head. Be aware of it in the processes of your inner organs and in the death and renewal of all the cells of your body. Feel how being here emanates from a source, a life force, a dynamic and ever-present stillness that creates and sustains you in every moment.

Five

Being Here

∽

There is nowhere to go. What you are looking for is right here.
Open the fist clenched in wanting and see what you already
hold in your hand.

Sometimes, anywhere else but where we are seems to be the place we need to be in order to stand a chance of finding real peace and inner stillness.

In the spring before I go out on my vision quest I am invited to go with a group to visit and study with the Shuar people in the Amazon. The Shuar are reportedly the only indigenous tribe in the Amazon never conquered by European colonialists. Given my life-long study of shamanism and my personal practices of earth-based ceremonies, I am drawn to the idea of going by canoe into the Amazon to study directly with one of the few peoples who, despite the encroachment of modern technology, are still practicing shamanism in a traditional manner in the context of a tribal culture living close to the earth. I am hoping the shamans of the Shuar will know how to do it differently, how to live exclusively from the peaceful presence I know myself to be at the deepest level. I hope that the wisdom and practices these people might offer me will provide useful guidance in how to prepare for and where to focus my intent during my vision quest.

The invitation is extended to me a week before the trip is to leave. I am tired from traveling for speaking engagements, but, in addition to wanting to take advantage of the opportunity to learn, I like the idea of spontaneously saying yes to an adventure without all the weeks of detailed preparation I would normally feel were necessary. I like the idea of doing something unpredictable and out of character. I want to take the invitation as some kind of sign that I am "meant" to go even though I know and have warned others about the tricky business of giving our choices over to easily misinterpreted environmental cues.

Sometimes it's hard to tell the difference between following deep intuitive guidance and being led around by the nose of unconscious wanting and fear. At an earlier point in my life I would have just said yes and buried any qualms I might have in the rush of logistical details required to get ready. The truth is it is probably going to be a wonderful trip. One way or another I will learn something, probably different although not necessarily more important things than what I would learn by staying home. But when I sit down and do my prayers and meditation, repeatedly asking whether or not it is appropriate for me to make this trip at this time, I receive the same answer over and over again.

I want to say something here about asking for this kind of guidance. Generally speaking, I don't think God or the Beloved or the Great Mother—whatever name you give to that infinite mystery that sustains us—cares a great deal about the little details of our lives. I don't think the Great Mystery, that consciousness that is both what we are and the source of what we are, cares whether or not I go to the Amazon or stay home because the consciousness that is larger than we are never forgets that it is not where we go or what we do but the level of awareness we bring to our actions that determines whether or not we are fully living our life purpose. So when I pray for this kind of guidance I am not so much asking whether or not the Great Mystery wants me to go to the Amazon. I am asking for help in discerning my real motivations and perhaps unconscious agendas and whether, given these motivations and agendas, this trip will help me wake up more fully or is just one more way of distracting myself from being present, one more way of trying to go back to sleep. I am asking, given who I am, whether or not this trip serves the larger purpose of learning to be fully who and what I am.

When I sit very still with these questions for an extended time, I hear in my mind's ear a small poem by Rumi, as it has been translated by Coleman Barks. It's a poem I have always found both appealing and challenging. I want to go on this trip. But every time I sit down to consider the trip, Rumi's poem runs through my mind like some tune I've heard on the radio and can't get out of my head. And Rumi says,

The mystery does not get clearer by repeating the question,
Nor is bought with going to amazing places.

Until you have kept your eyes
and your wanting still for fifty years,
you don't begin to cross over from confusion.

There are moments when I truly dislike this poem, but there is no denying the chord of truth it strikes within me. I don't need to go to the Amazon. That's not to say I should never or will never go. But making the journey in the hopes of finding something I think or am afraid is not where I am—here—is misguided, is in part a rejection of what is and a desire to change that situation. This would just be more doing. It's true that sometimes it is easier to hear or see what we are surrounded by when we are in an unfamiliar setting, not because what we are looking for is not available in the more familiar places, but because our seeing is sometimes more mindful when we are surrounded by the new. But the risk is that we get caught up in an endless need for novelty, spending all our time and energy moving about and searching instead of really seeing that what we are looking for is right here. We need a new way of seeing more than we need to see new things and places.

I have traveled to jungles, deserts, and wilderness areas throughout and beyond the North American continent to study with Christian, Hindu, and Buddhist teachers, yoga masters, and Native American elders. Some of the trips were grueling, most of them were enjoyable, and all of them offered me insight and inspiration. But I grew weary. It wasn't really the traveling that tired me out, although I have a physical constitution that doesn't recuperate easily from jet lag. It was the searching, the hoping that the next trip, the next sacred site or workshop or retreat, would offer a dramatic shift in perspective and I would finally find the secret to getting it right. I was pulling away from what was, letting my actions be determined by a desire to achieve a particular if unarticulated change. Aware of my tiredness, I stopped moving around so much, stopped studying and searching, and started sitting with myself and deepening my own practice, listening more carefully to my own conversations with the mystery within and around me. And yet even now, ten years after I have stopped attending most workshops or retreats, the lure of finding an answer elsewhere—this time in the Amazon—comes again.

> *Until you have kept your eyes*
> *and your wanting still for fifty years,*
> *you don't begin to cross over from confusion.*

For me this is most useful when I change it a little to read: *until you have been still with your wanting for fifty years you don't begin to cross over from the confusion.* What confusion? The confusion of thinking that what I am looking for is somewhere other than where I am. Why fifty years? Because it's too long to hang on, too long to pretend I am being still while reviewing where I have been and plotting where I might go next. It's not that it takes a long time, it's not that it takes any time at all. It's just that I have to convince my mind that there is no foreseeable end in sight if I am to really give up hope of getting somewhere. The idea of fifty years—of a long time—allows my mind to let go of attachment to achievement. The reality is that the moment I am completely with my wanting, the moment I am truly still with it and not trying to figure out a way to fulfill it or ignore it, it reveals itself to me. And I see and am with the fears that hook me into wanting things to be different from the way they are, fears that pull me into the belief that a different location or situation—a more creative job, a home in a more natural setting, more money or time or other resources, a relationship with someone who has the same "spiritual" goals or daily practice—is needed if I am ever to find deep abiding peace, if I am ever to learn how to love well. These beliefs are rooted in deeper if intermittent fears: the fear that I am not now and never will be able to hear the call at the center of my life accurately or fully enough to know how to consistently live who and what I am; the fear that the Beloved, tired of my inability to get it right, will simply stop calling, stop sending out the voice that can guide me home; the fear that I am not in the right place, have not found the right situation in which I can live my purpose fully, offer the one word I have come here to say and weave into the collective dream of the people.

This is what I learned on my quest: *There is simply no place, no location or situation, that cannot be used to wake up to and live all of what and who you are, if you are willing to show up, to be present in the only place you ever have access to: here.* Because what you long for, the awareness of the vast and sacred spaciousness at the center of what you are and the meaning it holds, is always here. Some situations or places will be more in alignment with your preferences. This may make it more pleasurable for you to be there, which may make it harder or easier for you to go to sleep to what and who you are and why you are here. But if our deepest soul's longing is to wake up and fully occupy the human life we have, and if we can do this any-where we are willing to be fully present, what then is this incredible attachment to and preoccupation with getting the details of our life situation to conform to what we want, to what we think is necessary or ideal for the satisfaction of this deepest longing?

• • •

Jeff and I are trying to decide where we will live after we are married. I rent a townhouse in downtown Toronto where I have lived for almost thirty years, although at this point I could do my work from pretty much anywhere. Jeff owns a townhouse in a small city about an hour west of Toronto and works about twenty minutes away from his home so needs to be in the general area to keep his job. We consider buying a place in the country near his work, but it is apparent that renovating his townhouse and living there would be much less expensive, so we decide that this would be the smartest thing to do. But as I stay there on weekends I can feel my resistance to living there. I do not feel at home in the suburban culture or aesthetic and am leery about trying to make ours a place that was his. After one difficult conversation the strength of my feelings becomes apparent, and we decide that regardless of financial considerations, living in Jeff's townhouse would not be a wise way to begin our life together.

And then something unexpected happens. Near the end of my forty days of ceremonial retreat I go to stay for a few days at Jeff's home. With Jeff at work all day, I stay with my routine of prayer and quiet introspection, and I begin to see the townhouse differently: the suburban streets are quiet, peaceful; the backyard is large and full of birds and squirrels and huge trees; the house is simple, available to be transformed with paint and care—and a lot of cleaning—into something that could feel like ours. After two days of sitting in this house, watching my own thoughts and feelings, being fully present and open to this place in a new way, I know that I could live here, could happily make this my home. I also know that I could be happy somewhere else—in a place in the country or staying in the heart of the city. From the perspective of being fully present, it really does not matter where I am. Each place has its challenges and gifts. When I am present each place is just *here*. It's the strangest feeling, very matter-of-fact, as if I have just stumbled upon something that is and has always been blatantly obvious, not an idea but a simple experienced truth. What matters is how we are together, not where we are.

The dilemma I have is this: if we really know, really experience, that the fulfillment of our deepest soul's desire to consciously be is not dependent upon where we are, how do we decide where to be? I mean, at any given moment we do decide to be somewhere in particular. On day thirty-nine of my time of prayer and introspection I sit with this question, and the Grandmothers of my dreams answer, "Be still and let the impulse to move come from deep within. Wait for it without waiting. Move when it comes." I know as they say it that to wait without waiting is to be still with yourself and the world, knowing that things will unfold without anticipating them, without taking yourself out of the present moment. I have a moment of wondering if this means we will be in the townhouse for ten days or ten years before a clear impulse to be elsewhere comes, but I know it does not matter.

On the last day of my forty days Jeff asks if I'd be willing to drive around in the countryside where we think we might look for a home to buy next spring, eight months down the road. Feeling that I will not be taken out of my meditative time, out of being present, if we set out, not with the intention of finding a house to buy but simply allowing ourselves to wander, I agree. Driving around, we see houses for sale, and I know, as I know with the townhouse, they are places I could be present and happy. I am curious but not anxious about how we will decide. Looking at a map of the area, I wonder out loud about a parcel of land where there appears to be a lake but few marked roads. We continue to wander and eventually find ourselves near this area on the map. Not realizing we are so close to what we find out later is a large wildlife preserve, we come upon a property for sale: a beautiful house with the privacy that will give us the quiet I love and the darkness Jeff needs to view the night sky through the telescopes he builds. The five-acre parcel of land has a large, deep, spring-fed pond and is surrounded by four hundred acres of forested conservation authority. We find the owner at home, and at the end of a three-hour visit with him, we buy the house.

This is what it is sometimes like when we are willing and able to really be here. When we let go of wanting things to be a certain way, when we let go of our certainty that we know how things should be, we find ourselves letting go of resisting or resenting what is true in this moment, truly at peace with what is often an unpredictable and sometimes messy human life. And in this acceptance we become a conscious participant in a larger flow. Awake to that flow, aware of the ever-changing and ceaseless movement of life, accepting of the ever-present cycle of birth and death and change, we are sometimes carried to a place that is filled with ease.

Talking about this is a tricky business. It can be a slippery slope from receiving and appreciating unexpected blessings to glib New Age platitudes about dreaming your own reality. Let's-make-a-deal beliefs fall too easily into formulas for using focused attention to earn what you want or to let go perfectly and can lead to blame and shame when things don't work out the way we wanted or thought they should. And you can't trick the universe into giving you what you want by pretending to be at peace with how things are, by imitating what you think it would look like to be fully present where you are, all the while looking over your shoulder to see if some higher power has noticed and is about to deliver you from where you are and put you where you really want to be. This is not a meritocratic system of reward and punishment. It's about coming into alignment with what is and, because what is is in a constant state of change, coming into alignment with that change, with that flow of life. Of course the flow of life, the wave of movement with which you come into alignment, may set you down someplace you could not have imagined. And in every situation, no matter what options life presents to you, the choice about how to be where you are—here—remains yours.

Would we have found and bought this same house if we had gone out industriously looking for a home that met a meticulously articulated list of criteria, if we had set up appointments with all the real estate agents in the area, examined conservation authority maps, looked at dozens of other houses, done our mantras and mudras and affirmations for the perfect home? Possibly. But the difference, the gift of the way it came to us, was ease. On the final day of the time I had designated as my quest, I had a direct experience of what the Grandmothers had told me to do on day six, of the very thing I was afraid I could never do: I tried, and found, easier. Ease brings with it a deep sense of peace and an innocent sense of delight and wonder. Ease allows us to be avail-

able to the possibility that real magic is possible in the interbeingness of reality. And ease can happen only when we are here.

For years I have been drawn to and yet challenged by another
Rumi poem translated by Coleman Barks that speaks to me of the
way of ease the Grandmothers advocate:

The Treasures' Nearness

A man searching for spiritual treasure
could not find it, so he was praying.

A voice inside said, "You were given
the intuition to shoot an arrow
and then dig where it landed,

but you shot with all your archery skill!
You were told to draw the bow
with only a fraction of your ability."

What you are looking for
is nearer than the big vein
on your neck! Let the arrow drop.

Don't exhaust yourself like the philosophers,
who strain to shoot the high arcs
of their thought-arrows.
The more skill you use, the farther you'll be
from what your deepest love wants.

—Rumi

What we are looking for is *nearer than the big vein in our necks* because what we are looking for is to be at peace with and live the purpose enfolded within our own human beingness. So trips to new and unfamiliar places are options, choices that may be distractions and are never necessities. Any place where we are present can amaze us, can be the place where we can find the treasure we seek. We can let the arrow drop and can dig anywhere because wherever we are is *here,* and that is the only place the treasure—a human life lived awake—is available.

How much human suffering, mine and others', comes back to our ambivalence about being here, our uncertainty about committing fully to a human life, to living awake with what is within and around us! And those of us who aspire to and cultivate the spiritual aspect of our lives may be particularly prone to living in the hopes of being elsewhere, if not externally than certainly internally. I have always been uncomfortable with spiritual teachings aimed at some form of transformation that would qualify me to eventually get to somewhere other than here, whether to heaven or to the mysteriously described state of formlessness. But the truth is that wanting to change myself, wanting to live only from an awareness of my essence and leave behind my ego, is every bit as much a rejection of being here now, because I can only be here now as a human being, as a being of ego and essence. The choice is whether I want to consciously be here or continue to fight with reality.

In the last few years, as my sons approached adulthood, I began to think about what my life would look like after they left home. I imagined living a more secluded contemplative life in an isolated location, spending long periods of time either alone or within a com-

munity dedicated to silence and contemplative prayer and meditation. I fantasized that under these conditions I would become a different person: a woman who did not feel and express herself so
strongly about world events or spiritual beliefs or would at least express her opinions only occasionally, gently, and with reticence; a
woman known for her calm, her balance, her quiet compassionate
nature. There are many people living in spiritual communities who
will tell you that changing location does not change who you are or
take you out of the relationship with others and the world.

For years it was love of my sons that stopped me from trying
to live out this particular fantasy of getting it right, of becoming (or
at least appearing) closer to perfect by living more "spiritually."
And now, as they are about to leave home, as the daily requirements of doing what needs to be done lighten, I am caught once
again by love. But to say I am caught is misleading. It's a choice. It
is always a choice about whether or not to commit to being fully in
the human life that is yours.

Jeff and I lost touch over the years, and then he tracked me
down three years ago and we fell in love once again. As we moved
closer to making a commitment to building a life and creating a
home together, I became aware of how entering this relationship
required a deeper commitment, a conscious willingness to choose
to be here, to accept my humanness. I have often jokingly said that
I am a completely sane and balanced woman when I am out of relationship and living alone. The truth is that I can more easily appear to myself and others to be a more sane and balanced woman if
I am alone. I can lead a more "spiritual" life when I don't have to
discuss mutual budgets and spending with someone else, when my

plans are not interdependent with another's, particularly when that other has forgotten to tell me some crucial detail about an upcoming event or is unhappy with how I have arranged things he asked me to take responsibility for in the first place.

Of course, this is not the whole picture, but it's the one I tend to focus on when I am fantasizing about the kind of life I want to lead and how much easier it would be if I were somewhere else. The truth is we are never out of relationship with others and the world, we are always interdependent with those around us. But I stand a much better chance of feeling like I am winning my fight with this aspect of reality if I am living alone, if I do not enter regular intimate contact with another, if I do not enter the container of committed relationship, if I do not open myself fully to loving and being loved.

Jeff and I are very different people. I trained in shamanism and mysticism, he trained in physics and engineering. At the beginning of a couples' weekend when each of us was asked to introduce ourselves using an adjective that began with the same letter as the first letter of our name, I introduced myself as "Ontologically Minded Oriah," and Jeff introduced himself as "Just Jeff." In my defense I want to say that I simply could not think of many adjectives that begin with the letter O (*ornery* was the only one that came to mind, and it revealed more than I wanted known so early in the workshop), and it's a little misleading to think of Jeff as "just" anything. He is a talented circuit board designer, astronomer, pianist, composer, and photographer. He is also a deeply intelligent thinker with a large, accepting heart who acquiesces to the limitations of being human with more grace and ease than I often display. Perhaps that's what makes it possible for him to love a woman who periodically thrashes about in her quest to do more and more when doing is not what is required.

Our relationship is a mystery to me. There are lots of good reasons to love Jeff, but none of them is why I am with him. Something simply drew me like gravity to be near him, the way a stone is drawn to the ground when it is dropped over a precipice from a great height. I cannot explain it. The cells of my body recognized something there near him that I needed. I was drawn to his solidity, his willingness to be here, his ability to see me in all my humanness and still love me steadily and fiercely. And sometimes fierce loving that endures thirty years of absence is what is required if you are going to love a woman who is sometimes so caught in her drive for spirit that she will forsake her own soul until it speaks to her in images of slit wrists and severed hands.

There may have been other men in my life who were willing to love me this way, but I had not been able to let love hold me, had not been ready to commit fully to a human life, to simply being here. In a human life love is tangible, incarnate, living within a heart made of pulsing muscle and blood, in a heart that will someday stop beating. To marry Jeff I had to make a choice to stop fighting with the reality of being here, of being human—both essence and ego—of living simultaneously the divine spark of what I am and the particular and not always endearing traits and tendencies of who I am. Marrying Jeff was a choice to say, I am here and it is good. Good is not perfect, but good is wonderful, as in full of wonder at how loving and being loved brings us more fully into our own lives, brings us more fully to the only place we can live who and what we are—here.

Meditation for Being Here

I am always surprised to find how often my attention is not on the
place where I am. Wanting to be here, I do a very simple and
short meditation throughout my day. It reinforces the more
lengthy practice I do at the beginning of each day. I do it
repeatedly wherever I am—in my car, at my desk, walking
outside—often when there is a lull in my normal activities, when I
am waiting for a stoplight, caught in a traffic jam, put on hold,
waiting for something to download into the computer. Each time
it brings me into full awareness of the present moment, of being
here.

   Wherever you are, as the thought comes to you, pause for a
moment in your daily activity and take three deep breaths. Inhale
through your nose and exhale through your mouth, letting your
weight drop down from your shoulders and upper body into your
hips and legs. On each exhale drop down a little farther and become aware of the surface beneath you that is supporting you.
Become aware of the places in your body where you are holding
on, and let go. You may want to pause gently at the end of the
next exhale, allowing the impulse to inhale to come from deep
within. Do not reach for it or resist it, just let it come and guide
your breath. Sit for a moment in the stillness in between.

   Be aware of where you are. Notice the quality of the light, the
feel of the air where it touches your skin, any scents or sounds
that are around you. Take it in as it is. Be here and let it be, and as
you continue on with your daily activity bring yourself back again
and again to an awareness of being here.

Six

Right Now

*There is no waiting for something to happen,
no point in the future to get to.
All you have ever longed for is here in this moment, right now.*

My friend Peter tells me about "weasel words." *Should* is the weasel word in the sentences "It should only take half an hour to install this new program in your computer" and "The renovation should be completed by the end of the week."

Just is the weasel word in the increasingly popular admonishment "You *just* have to be in the now." It implies that this is an easy and simple thing to do. My question is, why isn't it easy? Is it simply the nature of our minds to wander away from the present moment, to continually review, analyze, and judge the past or anticipate, worry about, or imagine the future? Certainly my mind does all of these, more or less continually. But surely the intelligent life force that has created so intricate and wonderful a universe would not make the one thing necessary for our liberation from suffering and ignorance dependent upon an ability we simply do not have or must struggle ceaselessly to develop. That would be like making our happiness dependent upon making a perfect jump shot and then making our maximum height two feet tall. Since I do not experience a hint of any such cruelty or sadism in the Beloved that calls me home, and I do experience an expanded ability to love well and accept my human life when I am fully present, I find myself searching for another explanation for why it is so difficult for us to be in the now.

Of course on one level we are always in the present moment. The past is gone and the future does not yet exist. Past and future, memories and dreams are ideas in our minds, ideas that are happening in the only moment we have access to: now. It's about being in the present awake, fully aware of this moment and what it holds. But for many of us our lives—our moments—are very full and very fast moving, making it difficult for us to see, let alone be, with it all. Discouraged by this, I imagine that I would have to live like an itinerant Zen monk to be fully present, and not all of us are suited or called to live a life of wandering solitude.

By the end of my forty days of ceremonial retreat, of long quiet periods of solitude and prayer and meditation, of slowing down and following the intuitive pull of the moment, I feel I have been shown and have learned a new way of living, a way of being more fully present with myself and the world. And then I am tested, plunged back into the waters of an ordinary human life. Oh, I'm not claiming that the Grandmothers or God or the Great Mystery set up the test, but life has a way of testing us particularly when we are feeling self-congratulatory about "getting" something. Or maybe it just feels like life is testing us when we notice that we seem to have lost track of what we thought we "got" so clearly only a moment or a day before. I get that the task is to continually be here now, fully with myself and the world. The challenge is to do this in a human life.

The day after my forty-day retreat is over life suddenly speeds up: having bought a new home, Jeff and I become embroiled in on-going exchanges and seemingly endless paperwork with mortgage brokers, real estate agents, and lawyers; there is a well to be tested, surveys to be found, inspections to be made; Jeff's place needs to be readied for sale and put on the market; we had already set our upcoming wedding date for October, so there is a wedding to plan for in six weeks; Nathan, my younger son, receives notice that he can have a place in the university residence if he moves in immediately, so in twenty-four hours we pack him up and move him in. All of this, of course, just as I am to start writing this book, writing that I have been mulling and anticipating doing for the last year. I know that writing a book about hearing and heeding the call at the center of our lives has to be done while hearing and heeding the call at the center of my life—the call to remember why I am here, to be consciously aware of the Sacred Mystery within and around me, and to let my actions flow from the silent knowing of this spacious center. There can be no separation between what I am writing and how I am writing it. So I do not wait for things to slow down, I do not seek to write in isolation, I start to write in the midst of an increasingly messy human life.

And things just keep accelerating. Today, two months later, I am writing a chapter about being in the present moment. But before I sat down this morning to ponder the now, I called the telephone company, propane supplier, post office, electric company, and Internet server to ensure upcoming services in our new home. I contacted the lawyer about signing papers next weekend, finalized the details of a new bank account, called the folks at the home insurance company, and tried to find a buyer for my piano. All of this, of course, in preparation for the move in five weeks. I am surrounded by the chaos of half-sorted closets, labeled boxes, and piles of things to be given away or sold. At the same time, the other demands of life continue. I answered twenty-four e-mails this morning, talked to my son about a paper he is writing on the relationship between the God of Genesis and our human frailties, and set aside an hour to call a woman I know who is ill in the hospital, feeling guilty that I am not going to see her, wanting to offer some comfort in a difficult time.

It is tempting to simply give up on being mindfully present until we have moved and settled into the new home. But when I review the last few years, although there have been few periods quite this full and chaotic, I can see the pattern of wanting to wait until circumstances change before I turn my full attention to simply being here. Although the particulars change, the pattern does not. I thought it would be easier to be present when I finished the book tour for the last book, when I was home more and things slowed down. But then I was drawn to write this book, and there was the wedding and the impending move. Before that I told myself I would slow down once the previous book was finished, but then, of course, I went on the book tour and was fortunate enough to be offered a number of speaking engagements. I can trace the postponement of consciously being present back for years like this through periods of waiting to finish a course, anticipating a child growing into the next stage of independence, or looking forward to the completion of a work project. And, of course, in the meantime life is going by and I am not fully in it. I am too busy doing.

Slowly it begins to dawn on me that this is it. This is the way life is: sometimes fast, sometimes slower, but always filled with both a multitude of daily requirements to keep life and limb together and a thousand other things we choose. Sometimes plans do need to be made, and the focus of plans, by definition, is on something—a meal, a gathering, a move—that is not happening now, that will happen in the future. But the plans—making the list, calling the phone company, packing a box—like everything else happen in the only moment we have access to: now. The trick is to pack the box without simultaneously reviewing the conversation I just had with the telephone company representative and making a list of what I have to do tomorrow. The task is to just pack the box or just type these words or just speak to the service person on the phone in this moment, all the while keeping one part of my attention on the spacious stillness within. Both my personality and my culture take pride in multitasking skills, but if we cannot bring our full attention to the present moment when we are doing one thing, it is doubtful that we will be able to do so when we are simultaneously doing three. Multitasking and mindfulness are, for most of us, mutually exclusive. Of course, doing one thing at a time will probably slow things down.

The minute I bring my full attention to this moment, letting go of mentally keeping track of what has happened or needs to happen next, I become aware of my body. I feel my breath and the stiffness in my back and remember that I have not done my yoga yet this morning. I let my shoulders drop. I am aware of my tiredness and the fear that it won't all get done or I will get sick getting it done or I'll forget something critical. And if I stay present with these feelings, letting my hands pause as they pack a box or move over the keyboard and just take three deep breaths, I am aware of another feeling that I do not want to touch, a feeling of something welling up inside me that I have been keeping at bay for weeks.

Herein lies the answer to my question *Why is it so difficult for us to bring our full attention to the present moment, to be here now?* Because there are aspects of reality we do not want to accept, that we cannot avoid being with if we are present.

I have lived in this city for thirty years. I have given birth to and raised my sons here. I have helped build and participate in a community of friends and students who have a shared history of spiritual practice and ceremony not easily found or quickly created elsewhere. Leaving this place means leaving what is familiar and loved, means leaving my friends, means leaving my sons. My younger son, Nathan, is living in the residence at the university near the northern edge of the city and has been coming home every weekend. He will not be able to do this as frequently at my new home. My older son, Brendan, attends a downtown university and lives at his father's townhouse eight doors away from mine, so I see him several times a week. His schedule of daily classes and weekend employment means he will be able to make only infrequent visits to my new home. They are nineteen and twenty-two, old enough to be on their own, particularly with the ongoing love and support they will continue to receive from both their father and me. Why then does my chest ache so when I come fully into the present moment, when I pause and look at the photographs I am packing, pictures of two small boys laughing in Halloween costumes or hunting Easter eggs, faces smeared with chocolate?

Other people tell me that the move is well timed, that it will increase my sons' independence, my freedom, and their ability to move more deeply into their own lives, and I know they are right. But it is the women whose children are slightly older than my own, the women who have recently moved out of what was the family home or have seen their children leave in the last year or two, who look at me silently and nod knowingly, their eyes suddenly shining with held-back tears. They know the sense of loss that rips through me now. I want to slow it down. I want to remember it all: the feel of their bodies, heavy and sweet, as I carried them to bed when they were small; the high-pitched squeals and laughter as I chased them up the stairs; the love, the fierce arguments. I want a chance to make up for all the ways in which I was not the parent I wanted to be, all the times I was too busy, too tired, too wrapped in my own fears for the future to love them well.

Years ago I heard someone quote the Zen master Suzuki Roshi: "We don't need to learn to let go. We just need to recognize what is already gone."

This is the reality we must face in every moment we are present: the reality of impermanence, the reality of continual change, the reality of loss that sits at the center of a human life. No two nows are the same. It is not that we lack the ability to be present. It is that we move away from it in our desire to deny or at least minimize the experience of change and loss that is life. In our war with the reality of impermanence, we move away from the now and so lose access to the essential and infinite stillness within, which could sustain us when those losses are painful. To live in the now we have to end our war with this reality, we have to accept the perpetual losses, small and large, that are a consistent part of what it is to be human.

A dear friend going through change too big to ignore in her life tells me, "I hate change!"

And I think to myself, this is the same as saying "I hate life!" or "I don't want to be in a human life!" Life as a human being is constant change, and because we love as human beings, change brings with it a sense of loss. And if we move away from this pain by moving away from the present moment, we miss the lives we have been given.

As I come into the present moment and feel my own grief over the current change in my life, I keep thinking I must be doing something wrong. After all, this is change that is chosen and good. Jeff and I have found a wonderful home in a setting that feeds my desire to live with more awareness of the earth beneath me. I want to live there, and I want to live with him. My sons are doing well, and I can continue to support them from a distance and see them regularly. Sons must leave their mother's house and go into the world. I do not wish for this to be different. I keep thinking that if I were doing it "right," if I were more "spiritual," I would not be feeling this grief. I keep thinking that if I could accept the reality of impermanence once and for all, I would not feel this ache.

Living in the now does not mean ending the war or surrendering to what is *once and for all*. Wanting *once and for all* is part of what pulls me into the war in the first place. It's about letting go of wanting once-and-for-all solutions that we think will extend through time into imagined futures, about ending the war I am fighting with reality in the only moment I have access to it—this moment—with this breath, this inhale I am taking right now as my fingers move on the keyboard, this exhale that leaves my body . . . this impulse to inhale again. . . . And when I end my war with impermanence, when I stop pushing away the loss that is, I am fed, supported, and sustained by an awareness of the still spaciousness within that can hold and be with it all.

Sometimes the losses in our lives are larger and harder than the change brought about by grown sons leaving home.

Leslie is a forty-year-old woman who has been living with cancer for over ten years. I met her when she first came to some talks I gave in 1986, and I have seen her occasionally since. Her cancer has advanced. She has a wound that will not heal in her groin, she cannot feel her legs completely or walk unassisted, and there are blood clots in her arteries the doctors fear will go into her lungs. I go to see her, to sit with her for a time. We laugh and talk about our lives, and then, after a few minutes of shared silence, she asks me what I think she should do. The doctors can recommend no treatment that will promise a cure. One course of treatment may prolong her life but will cause pain while another will make her more comfortable but is almost guaranteed to shorten her life. She does not want to die. She has investigated alternative treatments, some of which are costly and difficult to get, none of which can guarantee recovery. She must also choose whether or not to remain in her own home, with a succession of volunteers coming to help when they can, or to go to a hospice or to stay with family where there will be constant care.

She tells me about her fear and confusion and looks at me now, bewildered. "How do I decide?" she asks. "How do I know what course of treatment to take, where the best place for me to be is? I want to live, so should I keep fighting, keep trying anything that has any chance of prolonging my life? When is it okay to let go?"

I sit for a moment and feel both her tiredness and her desire to live. When I answer, I speak slowly, feeling my way into what I know is true. "I can't tell you what to do because I don't know what you should do. But . . . I do think that it is always okay to let go, to stop fighting with what is and just be with it. The truth—what is—is that you are very ill and we don't know how long you have or what the quality of that time will be. No one can know this for you or for ourselves—not you or me, not the doctors or the alternative health care practitioners." I pause and wait, feeling my breath moving in and out of my body before I continue. "But I have incredible faith in your ability to know for yourself what you need to do in this moment. If you can sit with the not knowing, with the fear and confusion and uncertainty that it raises, if you can really be with it, just breathing, just being, you will know if this is a moment to try a treatment or to simply be still. I think this has to be a present-moment decision, not a choice you make once for the rest of your life, however long that may be. If you can be present, with yourself, you will know if you need to breathe through the pain or ask for pain medication. You will know if you need to be at home or if you need to go where there will be someone with you all the time. And what is true right now—what is the best choice for you in this moment, today—may not be true, may not be what you need tomorrow. Today you may want to be still and present, just resting without doing anything. Tomorrow you may want to say,

'Bring on the treatment!'—may want to try something that may or may not work the way you hope it will. All I know for sure is that if you can take the time you need to find the deep stillness within and make your choice from that stillness, you cannot make the wrong choice, you can only make the choice that is the best one for you at the moment."

What is true for Leslie is true for all of us, although it is sometimes clearer when we are faced with life-threatening illness. Here is the only place and now is the only moment in which to look for how to live who and what you are. Going home, knowing who and what we are and why we are here, is not something we have to earn by getting it right, choosing perfectly, or trying harder. Sometimes work is required, sometimes pain is endured. Loss is an inevitable part of being human. The reality we live is impermanent, constantly changing. Leslie has had the fact of her mortality shoved up against her face, but the truth is none of us knows how long we have here. To be human is to be mortal, is to participate in constantly changing inner and outer realities.

Knowing this, facing the impermanence of our reality, we may be tempted to move away from loving deeply to protect ourselves from feeling the inevitable losses so acutely. But that would simply be fighting another aspect of the reality of being human, the reality of loving fiercely, of appreciating deeply and so being attached to the beauty we experience with the people and places and things we love. Being human means we are not detached, we are deeply connected to and affected by life.

Mary Oliver, in her poem "In Blackwater Woods," writes about the choice we have to make if we are to live present in a human life, in this constant cycle of life and death in our lives.

In Blackwater Woods

Look, the trees
are turning
their own bodies
into pillars

of light,
are giving off the rich
fragrance of cinnamon
and fulfillment,

the long tapers
of cattails
are bursting and floating away over
the blue shoulders

of the ponds,
and every pond,
no matter what its
name is, is

nameless now.
Every year
everything
I have ever learned

in my lifetime
leads back to this: the fires
and the black river of loss
whose other side

is salvation,
whose meaning
none of us will ever know.
To live in this world

you must be able
to do three things:
to love what is mortal;
to hold it

against your bones knowing
your own life depends on it,
and, when the time comes to let it go,
to let it go.

—Mary Oliver

This is what it means to answer the call, to commit to being here in a human life, as a human being: *to love what is mortal,* to love what is unpredictably changing and impermanent, to love while being mindful that everything, every person, every place, every moment we love will change and pass, but to love anyway. And to love what you love fiercely, no-holds-barred, nothing held back, *to hold it against your bones knowing your own life depends on it,* knowing that the reality of who and what you are as a human being is inseparable from this body, this world, this life you claim and inhabit fully.

And when the time comes to let it go—and no one can ever predict or control when that time will come—*to let it go.*

I am in awe of our human capacity—of my capacity, your capacity—to do this, to choose to love deeply and fiercely, conscious of the impermanence of all that we love, and when the time comes, to let go. It is our human nature—that marriage of essence, the pure and sacred presence that is the source of and greater than the sum of all things, and ego, our individual preferences and attachments—that gives us the ability to do this. If we commit fully to being human, if we say yes to being here now, this is what it is like: to love, to experience loss, and to refuse to step away from the realities of love and loss by seeking to live a more "spiritual" life, by looking for a way to get it right, to do it perfectly. To answer the call, to find what we long for, to be who we are is to accept the beauty and the challenge of being here now.

Meditation on Impermanence

Sit in a comfortable position. Turn your attention to your breath, taking three deep breaths in through the nose and releasing them out through your mouth. Let your body drop. Feel your shoulder blades slide down your back. Let the weight in your body move down into your hips and legs, and be aware of the surface beneath you that offers you support. If thoughts or feelings or sensations come, just touch them briefly, acknowledge they are there, and then gently let them go, returning your attention to your breath.

Be aware of the things around you. If there are furnishings made of wood, remember how they were once living trees, and imagine in your mind's eye the death of these trees and the fashioning of these furnishings. If the items around you are made of different materials, imagine how they were formed—the process that changed raw materials of some sort into items of use around you. Imagine how these furnishings have or will change over time, becoming worn, finishes fading and being renewed, joints loosening. . . . Imagine a point sometime in the future when the decay caused by aging is more advanced and the material these items are made of begins to disintegrate . . . seeing the items around you as they will be in fifty years . . . a hundred years . . . two hundred years . . . changing . . . and finally gone.

Feel this same movement of change in your own body. Over an average lifetime all of our cells are replaced seven times. The body you have now is not the body you had twenty years ago, and it is not the body you will have in ten or twenty years from now. Feel the continual movement of decay and renewal in your body, the overall process of aging that leads toward death and decay. Allow whatever feelings that come to be there, simply noticing them and returning your attention to your breath.

Remember a time when you were feeling very different than you are in this moment. Perhaps you were anxious and now you are relaxed. Perhaps you were filled with joy and now you feel sadness. Remember the feeling as it was and how it changed, dissolved, and became something else, and know that what you are feeling right now will do the same, will change and pass.

Think of all that you appreciate—the people or situations in your life that you enjoy. Feel any resistance you may have to the knowledge of the perpetual change that will come to all of these. Let yourself relax into what is, into the knowledge of impermanence. Let this knowledge bring you fully into this present moment, into the only moment you have: now.

Seven

Going Home

You are wearing yourself out with all this searching.
Come home and rest.

Sometimes, even when we can hear the voice of the
Beloved beckoning us home, we hesitate. Even as we
ache to find that place of belonging to that which is larger
than ourselves, to the meaning in our lives and the sacred presence
within and around us, we resist the call that would take us there.
Sometimes we keep searching to avoid going home, to avoid facing
unspoken and unresolved feelings we may have about the reality of
living in this world, about the Sacred Mystery that creates and sustains this reality.

Sitting in prayer alone in the wilderness on the third day of my
vision quest, I wonder to whom I am praying. To what do I call?
The sacred presence that surrounds and sustains us excludes nothing, but how we name that to which we call shapes the answer we
receive, the home that welcomes us. Thinking of the stories I was
told as a child about God, I am surprised to find myself thinking,
"Not to the God of Abraham and Isaac. I will not call to a God who

would test a man's loyalty by asking him to kill his son on the altar of sacrifice."

I sit on the earth and remember the story of Abraham, of how he and his wife, Sarah, well past childbearing age, prayed to have a child, and Sarah gave birth to Isaac. Do you know what it's like when what you've wanted forever is right there in your hand, when the thing you thought was impossible happens? It's hard to believe, sometimes difficult to really receive. You celebrate and give thanks, but sometimes, somewhere deep inside, you wait for it to be taken away, for the power that brought the impossible into your life to say, "Oops, that was a mistake," and take it back. That's what I think happened to Abraham. He'd prayed for the impossible, and his prayer was answered. But I think he feared from the beginning that God would take away what had been given. Don't we all have reason to believe we are undeserving? Don't we all know of a thousand instances when we have failed to be kind or courageous? Abraham had sent his son Ishmael and Hagar the maidservant who bore him into the desert when Sarah gave birth to Isaac. Somehow Hagar had been worthy of sharing his bed and bearing his child but not worthy of being in his household once his wife had had a son. There are those in the world still angry about that abandonment. Did Abraham think of Hagar and Ishmael when he thought he heard God telling him to take young Isaac up the mountain and sacrifice him on the altar? Was it the voice of God, or was it the voice of fear, the voice that tells us that we are unworthy of the unearned blessings in our lives?

For years I prayed for the husband of my heart and hearth, flip-flopping between diligently searching and vowing never to date again. Eventually I came into a quiet acceptance of my aloneness, but still I longed for the intimacy of being seen and loved by another. And then there was Jeff.

During the winter before my quest Jeff and I decide to take a short trip and stay one night at a small inn north of Toronto. Exhausted from too much travel, I need to get to the wilderness. Arriving in the afternoon, we bundle up in long johns and layers of polar fleece and head out into the five thousand acres of wilderness that surrounds the inn. It's well below freezing. The air is crisp and clear. We walk side by side on the trail through the bush, listening only to the crunch of our boots on hard-packed snow.

Suddenly we come to a bit of a clearing. A cliff of gray granite topped with dark evergreens rises to our right, and the snow stretches out before us, unmarked and glistening. I stop walking and stand still in the dying light of the afternoon, watching small clouds of moisture drift through the cold air each time I exhale. And my weariness catches up with me. I feel an ache run through my limbs, a pull to take my body to the earth for rest, to soak in the silence of the wilderness and let it wash away the bone-deep fatigue caused by too many anonymous hotel rooms and too few quiet moments on unpaved earth. Jeff stops next to me.

"I just need to do something for a few minutes," I say to him. Unable and unwilling to offer more explanation, I lie down, stretching out on my back on the snow-covered ground. I let my tiredness take me and the earth hold me. I let go of all the places where I have been holding on, all the places where I have been getting ready for the next round of airport lineups, bookstores filled with unfamiliar expectant faces, and conversations with friendly inquiring strangers. Tears of relief slowly trickle from the corners of my eyes, hot against my cold skin.

Jeff stands for a moment and watches me. "Are you okay?" he asks quietly. I nod. He waits for a moment, and then he does the one thing that lets me know he is indeed the mate for whom I have prayed for so many years. Later I think of other men I have loved and imagine what some of them might have done. Some of them probably would have become anxious and concerned that I would catch cold, insisting that I get up right away. Some of them would have walked on slowly and perhaps waited for me up ahead. Some of them would have called me crazy, and at least one of them, a therapist, would have knelt down and asked well-meaning questions, hoping to help me "process" whatever emotions were moving through me.

All understandable responses. But Jeff did none of them. Jeff just lay down next to me, stretching out on his back in the snow, his shoulder lightly touching mine, silently watching the sky with me.

Do you know what it's like when what you've wanted forever is right there in your hand, when the thing you thought was impossible happens? I imagine now that I know how Abraham felt, how he anticipated having that which was so precious to him taken from him. For the first time, on the third day of my vision quest, I realize yet another of my unconscious motives for being out here in the wilderness, determined to stay and pray and fast for forty days. I am afraid that God—the God of my childhood, the God of Abraham—will find me unworthy of the blessings in my life. I want to prove to this God that I have not grown complacent, am not taking for granted the good fortune that has befallen me. I want to pay for what I have been given so it will not be taken away. I want to be worthy of a love that survived thirty years of absence, worthy of a man who will lie down in the snow with me in subzero temperatures, no questions asked, and just silently feel the earth and watch the sky with me.

I am neither a theologian nor a biblical scholar. I am sure that wiser minds can offer more erudite explanations for the story of Abraham and Isaac. But as I sit here alone in the bush praying and meditating, the story comes to me now and offers me an awareness of some of my own unconscious fears, and for this I am grateful. I have not thought of this story in years, but I remember that even as a child I could never quite believe that the voice Abraham heard demanding that he sacrifice his son to prove his loyalty to God was in fact the voice of God. It was just too inconsistent with my experience of the presence that was within and around me, the Sacred Mystery that has always said to me in a thousand ways, "Live!" Sometimes sacrifices are required. A choice for one thing often means leaving another option behind. Sometimes we must give up our attachment to our ideas of how things are or should be in order to hear that which is larger than ourselves speak. But these are sacrifices not *of* life but *for* life, choices that don't come close to the spirit of sacrificing an innocent child to prove blind obedience. If God had any part in that story I think it was in providing the young goat for the sacrifice so that Abraham's fears and feelings of unworthiness did not result in his son's death.

I sit with my own mixed motives and viewpoints. I experience and know the Beloved to be a consistent source of loving grace, and yet I come out to the wilderness unconsciously hoping to placate the God that demands blood sacrifices just in case such a God exists? Am I hedging my bets, or do I really believe and experience the Sacred Mystery as unconditionally loving?

The question forms a small hard knot of anxiety in my stomach. My hands begin to sweat. I get up and begin to move around my campsite. A spark of something dark and forbidden runs through my body like a small electrical shock, a pinprick of fire. My jaw clenches, and the muscles of my arms and legs contract in what I realize is anger. I begin to pace and ask out loud, "What am I so angry about?" Allowing the anger I so often repress or deny to wash through me, I feel images of outrage carried on a wave of heat. I am angry about a lot of little things: my son once again removing my TV remote's batteries to power his video game; the garbage being put out before the cat litter is cleaned; the person who repeatedly puts her car in my parking spot; Jeff's lack of awareness that laundry can be done—in an automatic washing machine, eliminating the need to go down to the river and beat it on a rock—before every single piece of clothing and household linen is filthy. But I am also angry about the big things: the deaths of ten thousand children every day from starvation when we have the means to feed the world; the shortsightedness and greed that prompt some to maximize private profit at the cost of poisoning the water and air and earth that sustain us all; leaders who convince men and women to sacrifice their sons and daughters in wars launched in the name of freedom or democracy when they or their predecessors have begun or used armed conflicts to acquire or increase their own power and wealth. As I pace with the particulars, letting the feelings rise from my belly, I feel a deeper level of anger that fuels my smaller frustrations, a kind of ever-present rage that colors my view of the world, affects my desire and ability to go home to the Beloved I know and rest.

I am angry with God.

I am angry at the sacred and mysterious life force that has created and sustains this world. Why create a place where incredible suffering is possible and probable, where we can and often do choose to do great harm to ourselves and each other? Why not create us as fully enlightened beings, knowing from the start who and what we are, capable only of loving well and being fully present? For the lessons we can learn? When I hear about a ten-year-old child in my city being beaten to death by his parents after years of being abused, after being made to eat his own vomit as a punishment for throwing up in fear, I don't give a shit about preserving free will or valuing the lessons learned. I just want it to stop! And I am angry at that which is larger than myself for allowing it to go on, for creating and sustaining a reality where such injustice and suffering is possible in the first place. What kind of loving intelligence would allow such suffering?

Filled now with a rage that frightens me, I cannot sit down. The ground is rocky and uneven and the trees too dense to allow me to run, so I begin to climb the cliff that rises behind my campsite, needing to exert myself physically. I scramble as fast as I can up the steep slope, clinging to trees perched on rocky outcropping until I come to a broad ledge and collapse exhausted. The rock face at my back is a mix of pink feldspar and creamy quartz, a rough surface of gleaming crystals set in light gray granite. All I can hear is the sound of my own ragged breath. Suddenly overwhelmingly tired, I lie down on the lichen-covered ledge. Slowly my breath returns to normal and I fall asleep there, high above the tops of the trees that surround my campsite, slipping into dreams, muttering a desperate "Why?"

And I dream. I am in a field of tall grass and wildflowers, the sun warm upon my back. One of the Grandmothers stands next to me and points to a figure in the distance. It is an ox, munching on the tall grasses and flicking flies away from its back with the lazy movement of its tail.

"What is the defining attribute of the ox?" the Grandmother asks me.

"Strength," I answer without hesitation.

She nods. "And does an ox know its strength if there is no cart to pull, if it has only long days of grazing in fields of grass?" She pauses. "Strength is its nature, and yet that nature is only revealed when it is called upon to do some necessary task." She turns to face me, her hand lightly touching my cheek, her eyes holding mine in their gaze. "If you were fully enlightened from the moment you arrived here, you would not know the fullness of love and compassion."

"Why not? Why not make us loving compassionate enlightened beings from the start?" I feel myself blush at how young and insistent my voice sounds.

The Grandmother drops her hand and laughs, "And to whom would you be extending that love and compassion, Oriah? If everyone was enlightened there would be no suffering, no need for compassion. Remember the ox and the cart. The only way for you to know what you are, to know your essential attribute, is for you

to be in a position where you have to use that attribute, test it, feel
its strength, its power to heal where healing seems impossible, to
move where all forces seem immovable, to comfort when despair is
beyond comfort. . . ." She looks around the bright field and surrounding forest, inhaling a deep breath of the sweet fragrances that
surround us, and brings her eyes back to mine, smiling. "This is
what you are, this capacity to let love act in the world through you,
and this world is the place you can realize what you are fully."

"So suffering is created so we will know how to love?"

"No," she replies, a touch of sadness in her voice now. "Suffering is not created. It is allowed. You have free will."

I cannot help myself. "But what's it all for? If the suffering we
are allowed to create helps us discover what we are at the deepest
level, lets us experience our capacity for love and compassion, does
this all bring something larger to fruition, is it for some higher purpose?"

The Grandmother shakes her head at my mental gymnastics.
"Oriah, love and truth and beauty, these things are attributes of the
mystery itself. Their realization is the point, is the purpose. What
can be higher than these? They are not a means to an end. Realizing them, living them, is why you are here, and this realization is
dependent upon your having free will, which you may not always
use wisely."

I wake up on the ledge feeling warmed by the sun in my
dream and slowly make my way down the cliff to my campsite and
sit by the fire pit. For years I have unconsciously skirted my anger
with God, afraid to acknowledge or feel my outrage at the suffering
the sacred life force allows to manifest in the world. And so long as

there is something within ourselves or the world that we cannot ac-knowledge and be with, we must keep moving, must avoid the deep stillness within and around us that is the home we long for. I could not go home and rest in the arms of the Beloved until I could face my rage. Now, my anger spent, I follow my breath and simply sit with what is: we have free will and often make choices that cause suffering. But we can respond to suffering with love and compassion, realizing our essential nature, what we are, as we do so. Without free will this would not be possible, and free will al-lows for the possibility of making serious mistakes. I cannot argue with this. I have known the reality of my own free will from a very early age.

I hesitate to tell this next story for fear of being considered by some to be a little crazy. But then it wouldn't be the first time that was true. All I can do is tell you what happened. I forgot about it for many years, literally did not think about it from the day after it happened until I remembered it when I was in my midtwenties. And then one day, walking into a store in downtown Toronto, I caught the scent of a woman's perfume as she passed me, and sud-denly I remembered. It was like recalling a place you have visited on holidays, the taste of papaya or the scent of the sea suddenly re-minding you of a very specific day you had there, a day that seemed unforgettable at the time. I was not prodded by an over-eager therapist or inspired by watching movies about the occult. In fact, I have never liked frightening movies, and at that point I had not done any therapy. At the time I told no one what I remembered and have told only a very few people since.

I am very young, probably no older than five. I am in my bed having said my bedtime prayers, those strangely macabre ones instructing God on what to do "if I should die before I wake. . . ." I am alone in the room and the door is closed. I like sleeping in the dark. I am feeling mildly upset about something. Perhaps I have been chastised for doing something wrong that day. Since I am a diligent rule keeper this is rare, but when it happens I take it to heart. Or perhaps I am picking up on some difficulty my parents are having, a disagreement or worries about money or my father's health. I don't remember. I do remember lying in bed feeling mildly anxious about something and suddenly noticing a strange smell in the room.

The smell makes me want to turn my face into my pillow and take shallow breaths, like the bitter smell of ether just barely covered with the scent of overripe apples or the cloying odor of an unwashed body almost buried beneath the strong fragrance of expensive perfume. It is sweet, too sweet, and makes my stomach turn. As the smell gets stronger my mouth is flooded with an acidic taste that makes me swallow, a metallic taste like the one you get when your fork touches a filling in a tooth or when you bite down on a piece of aluminum foil accidentally left on a piece of chocolate. The temperature in the room suddenly feels cooler. Shivering slightly, I snuggle down into the covers and pull my blanket up over my chin.

And then I hear the voices in my mind's ear. Like the scent, they too are sweet, too sweet, as if deliberately seeking to hide something unpleasant even as they offer comfort. Neither clearly male nor female, they tell me that if I go with them I will feel better and everything will be all right. Their tone hints at forbidden treats, holds the promise of a place that is warm and blissfully care-free, seeks to entice.

I feel my small body tense beneath the covers. I can feel the lure of what they offer as something that would feel wonderful, but I am suspicious, suddenly afraid that the pleasure would be short-lived and followed by something unpleasant, like candy that tastes wonderful but gives you a stomachache a half hour after it is eaten. Although I can feel the temptation to "go" with them, I suddenly know with great certainty that they are "bad" voices. I have the sense that saying yes to the voices does not mean that I will actu-ally go anywhere physically but that I will be declaring my intent and opening a door to being with these voices, to receiving their comfort and their presence continually for a very long time.

And so I pray. I say a prayer to the God of my Sunday school class, to Jesus as I imagine him from the *Children's Illustrated Bible* in my parents' living room bookshelf: a strong, kind man blessing the children under the trees on a sunny afternoon after someone else has complained that the children should be sent home because they are too noisy and rambunctious (one of my favorite stories); a man standing on the waters of a raging sea, his long hair being whipped around his face by the wind and the rain, holding his arms out to a small group of terrified fishermen being tossed about in a small boat, urging them to leave the boat and walk across the dark waves to him. I pray to God, to this Jesus, to protect me from the bad voices, to send them away. Even at five I have a clear sense of the presence of that which is larger than myself, and when I pray on this night that presence is there, steady and strong, lovingly with me.

But the message I get is clear: God cannot or will not send the bad voices away. Jesus can do nothing until I choose to say yes or no to the voices. The choice is completely mine. When I tell the voices I will not go with them, that they must leave, the presence I identify as God comes closer, and I imagine myself falling asleep held in a large and loving hand, as I have on many other nights.

For three nights in a row the "bad" voices come and ask me to go with them, and each night I call on the loving presence I know to be with me, and it is there but can do nothing, can offer me only a silent witness until I decide whether or not I will say yes or no to the voices. For three nights in a row I tell the voices "No!" and send them away. They have not returned since that time.

Remembering this story as a young adult, I am amazed that I ever forgot such a vivid experience. It does not feel like a dream. I remember being wide awake, falling asleep only after the voices left. I am struck by how inconsistent this experience is with the gently sanitized Bible stories I was taught as a child. Being raised in a very liberal mainstream Protestant church, I can honestly say that I don't remember ever hearing about the devil. There was no talk of evil or Satan, and the demons cast out of another by Jesus were explained as illnesses that were healed. I had no name for the voices and told no one of my experience at the time.

The thing that bothered me most when I remembered this experience was the apparent unfairness of it all. Assuming for the moment that some sort of negative beings or energy did in fact visit me—since I choose to accept my own experience as real—how could a five-year-old child be expected to make a choice about whether or not to say yes to something seductively offering her comfort and relief from her small anxieties? This was completely contrary to my adult assumptions about the need to protect children from taking the consequences of serious choices. But my experience at the time had not seemed to me to be at all unfair. I knew the presence of God as a completely abiding love that simply would not interfere with my freewill choice. To my five-year-old heart and mind, not interfering with my freewill choice seemed completely fair, an expression of the depth of the love that enfolded and sustained me. Although I was tempted to go with the voices, to seek relief from my fears and anxieties in their promises, I did not feel incapable of making this choice. I knew the voices were "bad," and knowing this, I chose to send them away. It was my choice. It had to be.

This strange incident in my early life planted within me two seeds of certainty: that each of us is deeply and consistently loved by the mystery that is larger than ourselves, by the Beloved that is always with us; and that each of us is completely responsible for our choices. This does not mean we always make the right choice. I have made and will no doubt again make choices that have caused suffering for myself or others. In the *Tao-te Ching* Lao-tzu reminds us that the master trusts even those who are untrustworthy. Even knowing our human frailties, the Sacred Mystery endows us with free will and does not interfere with the choices we make. This is how loved we are. And no matter what our choices are, the voice of the Beloved still calls to us, still asks us to come home and rest.

Meditation on Spaciousness

My experience of the essential nature of all that is has as one of its
strongest qualities spaciousness, the sense that what I am and
what I am held by can include it all. Loosely based on a yoga
meditation I read years ago, this meditation sometimes has a
strange Alice-in-Wonderland feel to it, but it helps me tune in to
the reality of there being enough room for it all—for the moments
of wisdom and the moments of foolishness, for the anger and the
fear that sometimes keep me from going home, and for the
longing and the reassurance that sooner or later comes to get me.

Sit in a comfortable position. Take three deep breaths in
through your nose and out through your mouth, allowing your
body to let go of all tension and tiredness with each exhale. Let
your body drop down, and feel the support of the surface beneath
you and the earth beneath that surface. Let go of the places where
you are holding on.

Imagine your breath as a gentle hand, a ladle you can use to
scoop out the different parts of your body, leaving them open and
hollow inside. Breathe down into your feet—first one foot and
then the other—imagining your breath on the inhale scooping out
all but the outer layer of your foot. With the exhale imagine each
foot hollowed out, spacious and clear within. Repeat this process
with each leg, letting the inhale scoop out the inside of the leg
and the exhale simply dissolve all that was there. Maintain a sense
of hollowness and spaciousness inside those parts of your body
where you have directed your breath. Breathe into the pelvis and
abdomen, and imagine this part of your body becoming empty.

Breathe into your back—first the lower back and then the middle and upper back—filling the whole of your torso with light and air and feeling it become empty and spacious with the exhale. Breathe down into your hands and throughout your arms—the lower arms, elbows, upper arms, and up into the shoulders—allowing each breath to create an emptiness, a hollow sensation, in the center of your limbs. Breathe into your neck and throat, feeling the hollowness there, and up into your head, feeling a spaciousness opening up there with the exhale.

Sit for a moment breathing into the spaciousness of this hollow body you have created with your mind's eye, feeling the movement of air in and out of this spaciousness at the center of yourself. Then, with each breath, imagine the hollowness filling with light and air and expanding, your body becoming larger. Imagine the spaciousness and so too your body growing larger, becoming as large as the room in which you sit . . . and then as large as the building where the room is . . . sitting now, on a vast expanse of land as large as a city . . . and then as large as the country or continent where you are. Keeping the sense of inner spaciousness, imagine yourself growing to the size of the planet, and then larger . . . to the size of a figure sitting on the planet as if the earth were a meditation cushion . . . and then larger still. Feel within you the spaciousness that holds it all . . . all the stars and galaxies . . . every word and movement and feeling of every creature . . . and still there is spaciousness, a vastness that could hold much more. Sit with this feeling, and breathe into the vast emptiness.

Then, when you are ready, begin to let yourself grow smaller, always keeping the sense of spaciousness within. On the exhale, feel yourself once again the size of the earth . . . the continent . . . and then the country . . . and the city or area where you are. Exhaling, come down to the size of the building you are in or the trees around you . . . the room you are in . . . and back to what you perceive as your normal size. Breathe here, continuing to feel the spaciousness within you. Exhaling again, feel yourself grow smaller, becoming the size of a cushion . . . and then the size of a drinking glass, all the while keeping within yourself the awareness of the spacious emptiness within you. Exhale and feel yourself become the size of an apple . . . an acorn . . . a mustard seed. Sit with this sense of smallness and within this a sacred emptiness that can hold it all. Feel how, even imagining yourself as small as a mustard seed, you have within you room for galaxies and worlds, space for all the ever-changing feelings and thoughts and sensations to pass through. Sit with this.

When you are ready, on each inhale begin to grow, gradually returning to what you perceive as your normal size, keeping the sense of hollowness, of emptiness at the center of your body. Gradually open your eyes and begin to move through your day with a sense of how what you are can include it all.

Eight

Surrender

How much longer can you live like this?
Your hungry spirit is gaunt, your heart stumbles. All this trying.
Give it up!

It is December 2001. I am attending an evening of song and dance at my younger son's high school for the performing arts. I am here to support Nathan, happy to do so but not expecting to receive much from the evening. Like most parents, I have sat through many long and sometimes tedious school performances, applauding the efforts of teachers and students and patiently waiting to go home. But this night, beginning as it does with a small group of young men and women coming onstage to do some traditional African drumming, promises more.

According to the United Nations, Toronto's population comes from a wider diversity of ethnic origins and nationalities than any other city in the world. There are over seventy different languages being spoken in the halls of my son's school. Watching the drummers, young men and women of every color and creed, led by a young black man from Africa, play the traditional rhythms of tribal peoples makes me smile. The drummers are joined by fifty or more students, including my son, all in different-colored T-shirts, arrayed like a giant rainbow across the stage. They sing an African folk song first in its original language and then in English, singing, "We are walking, we are walking, we are walking in the light of God." As I watch them I think of the Native American prophecy that it will be the Rainbow Peoples, the children of mixed blood and ways, that will help the world find a way to live in balance when the center appears to no longer hold and chaos flourishes.

The end of the evening delivers what the beginning promised.

The stage is dark and silent, and as the lights slowly come up the audience sees a group of about twenty-five students, all dressed in light brown bodysuits that make them appear vulnerably naked and akin to each other. Their bodies are unmoving, intertwined on and around large wooden boxes stacked on stage. The light shining on the tower their bodies create is bright and harsh. The music begins with a loud guitar riff that grates on the ears and the nerves like nails across a blackboard. The voice of a newscaster reporting that two airplanes have just hit the twin towers of the World Trade Center in New York blasts into the auditorium over the loudspeakers. Lights begin to flash, sirens scream, and the smoke of dry ice slides across the stage and rises, billowing around the dancers. A shiver of recent memory runs through the audience. It has been burned into our mind's eye: the image from the TV played over and over of the plane flying into the office tower, balls of orange flame and black smoke exploding against a clear blue sky. The dancers scatter, writhing and falling, frantically running and carrying each other. It's difficult to watch, impossible to look away. I hear a woman sitting close to me begin to sob. It's hard to breathe.

Slowly the sirens fade and the air clears. A steady blue-white light starkly illuminates the stage. Some of the dancers wander dazed amid the bodies of others scattered on the floor. Slowly, as the Beatles song "Come Together" washes over us, the dancers begin to move to the rhythm, whirling and spinning, lifting each other up, coming together in pairs and small groups, slowly climbing back onto the large wooden boxes to form a tower of human bodies once again. But this tower is different, not immobile and silent but moving, alive. As the dancers simultaneously make two short movements expanding outward followed by two more pulling inward, the whole tower pulses in and out as the sound of a human heartbeat fills the auditorium. The sound fades, the lights dim, and we sit silent together in the dark, stunned by the beauty created from such suffering.

Slowly, softly, the school band begins to play another Beatles song, "Let It Be," and the stage and auditorium aisles fill with young men and women of every possible ethnic origin and religious background holding candles and singing together.

I have been part of and watched many healing ceremonies and memorial services commemorating the tragedy of September 11, but none have affected me the way this small high school performance did. Perhaps because it was so unexpected. Perhaps because it was our children who offered us this, an image of life that is profoundly touched but not destroyed by the shock of violence, by tragedy and loss. I could feel it in my own body and in the bodies of those sitting around me: something we had been holding had been released. Our sons and daughters had offered us a way to stop pulling away from what was, and in letting go of our resistance to the grief and the pain, our awareness of a sacred stillness that could hold it all flooded into the space created. And we were simply able to let what already was, be.

All the way home I kept thinking about the phrase *let it be* and how much less confusing I find it than being advised to let go. Letting go sounds like something we have to do. There have been a thousand times in my life when I have been clear that what I needed to do was surrender, to let go. And I couldn't do it no matter how hard I tried or prayed or declared my intention to do so. I thought it was an act of the will, something I could do, and I didn't know how. Only now do I understand that letting go, surrendering to what is, is a kind of not-doing, a stopping, letting things be. When I surrender I stop doing something I am already doing. I stop resisting what is. I stop following thoughts and feelings and sensations into unconscious doing aimed at fulfilling the desire to make things different than the way they are. And in the space created by this stopping, if I am present, an experience of what I am and why I am here fills me. The phrase *let it be* reminds me that I cannot change what has happened by pulling away from grief and fear, cannot erase what is by refusing to be with it, can only let things be as they are and in this stopping provide an opening where the action that flows from the center of my being can find me.

In the fall of 2001 I traveled to many American cities on a previously arranged book tour. And everywhere I went people asked me, "What do you think we should do?" seeking my opinion on military action or domestic measures aimed at ensuring future safety.

And every time I was asked I said the same thing: "I don't know. But I do know that if we can sit together, if we can truly be together without moving, without seeking to pull away from or act upon our feelings—the grief, the fear, the anger—and the enormity of what has happened, I have faith that the wisdom we need to take action, to move, will come to us."

Nowhere were people more receptive to this suggestion than in New York City. Over and over I heard, from the people who were most directly affected, the desire to find a way to be still, to sit with all that had happened and the thoughts and feelings that were still, months later, catching them off guard. One of what is called the Heart Laws of the shamanic tradition in which I was trained says, *Life chooses life.* In the midst of so much anguish, in the aftermath of life-destroying violence, the impulse, the often unspoken hunger that arose in so many, was to find that sacred stillness that would allow the wisdom they needed—the wisdom their community needed—to find them. This is life choosing life, this longing to be still, this impulse to stop, to wait until movement comes from deep within and not from the frantic and fearful voices within or around us.

But finding a way to sit still and be in the midst of a culture that values and pushes for speed is not easy. Over and over I heard from people who felt pushed to continue, to accelerate their doing after September 11. Sometimes this push came from inside themselves. Doing kept them in motion, one step ahead of the grief and terror they feared would swallow and immobilize them if they sat still and let it catch up with them. We have so little faith in the human heart's capacity—our capacity by virtue of what we are—to hold it all. We have to cultivate this faith by sitting with what is when what is is simply the small daily trials. We need to practice being present and still with ourselves when it is not so difficult if we are to stand any chance of being with the truly hard things when they happen.

To many, doing seemed imperative after September 11. There were so many people in need. Many of those I spoke with in New York were helping people directly affected by the tragedy to find homes and jobs. How could they follow their longing to stop doing, to be still, when the needs were so real? We do not have faith that if we could simply be with what is, the actions that would flow from this all-inclusive stillness would take care of all that truly needs to be done. And if we could be together the tasks would be shared, would flow from our collective body and so not burden and exhaust a few.

Doing was being urged not just by those genuinely concerned for people in need but by community leaders afraid that the economy would stumble and fall. I think they were afraid that if this tragedy shocked people into slowing down and reevaluating their lives, too many might stop pursuing activities and commodities that were failing to fill the hole felt at the center of too many lives. If such a realization were widespread it could indeed have far-reaching effects on profits and the economy of the community. But do we want the physical well-being of our families and communities to depend on convincing people to acquire more and do more by holding out the false promise that material acquisition and goal fulfillment can replace real meaning in our lives? While achieving goals can bring temporary satisfaction, it can never replace the need to know the meaning found in experiencing what we are. I heard one politician urge Americans only days after September 11 to "Show the terrorists that they cannot shake our core American values. Get out there and spend and buy and invest!" Perhaps if we could simply be together we might discover that as human beings these are not really our core values after all.

One woman in New York told me, "I feel as if the whole country is saying to us, 'Get back to normal, get moving, keep going,' when all I want to do is stop."

I asked her, "If not for this, what would you stop for?"

Even with the best motives, because doing is always a tensing up against and a resisting of what is, because it refuses to take more than minimal satisfaction from the process itself and is overwhelmingly attached to achieving specific results, because it cannot easily stop or change direction when new information—internal or external—is available, it takes tremendous energy and is not sustainable. New energy, new resolve, motivation, and enticement must be found to continue. Some things can be achieved by doing, but the cost is very high, and the achievements fortify our belief that we must keep doing, taking us further and further from the essential stillness we long to find, luring us into exclusively identifying with and relying upon our ego's ability to do.

Doing wears us out. I used to think that when I collapsed in exhaustion after once again doing too much—even when what I was doing was by choice and seemed valuable—that I was surrendering, letting go. But collapsing physically and emotionally is not surrendering. Surrendering has to be a conscious choice. Collapse is a temporary defeat often fueled by despair, a momentary lull in our doing while we seek to restore energy and gather enough resources to go back out and attack whatever situation we think needs to be other than the way it is. This is true whether the situation I seek to change by doing it right is internal, like wanting to do whatever is needed to live more often from my inner stillness, or an external set of circumstances in the world.

The great teacher and Indian leader Mahatma Gandhi believed that if we refused to cooperate with the institutions and practices that perpetuated injustice and violence by embodying a practice of nonviolence in thought, word, and deed, we would melt the hearts of those who were supporting and maintaining those institutions and practices. He sought to become the peace he wanted to see in the world. He advocated holding this place of nonviolence without any attachment to the results it brought, fueled by a daily practice of connecting with an awareness of that which is larger than ourselves. What faith he must have had in our essential nature, in the presence that is within and around us! But I am not Gandhi. I am a woman too often caught in the desire to make things within myself and the world different than they are, a woman often exhausted by doing, a woman afraid that if we are not doing, the things that matter in our individual lives and the world will not get done. Often the best I can do is to watch and see where I lose the thread of awareness of my still and spacious center and fall into the unconsciousness of doing. Observing myself, I discover a warning light: I know that I am moving away from simply being and into doing when I feel a sense of urgency instead of a sense of gravity, the deep but gentle pull from the still center guiding me.

• • •

I have agreed to sit on a panel at a conference discussing our hopes and fears for the future of the planet. One of the other women on the panel, Janice, is a dedicated environmentalist. Her views about finding and developing alternative and sustainable technologies are ones I respect and share. She has at her fingertips much more information about the degradation of global resources than I do. Perhaps this burden of carrying and sharing information we all need to make wise choices is what fuels her sense of desperation. When she speaks you can almost see the fear pour from her body as she hunches over the microphone, can sense her desperate need to get the audience to agree with her assessment of the situation. Her voice becomes more high-pitched as she leans forward in her chair even farther and with real urgency pleads, "We are running out of time! If we don't do something right now to change things it will simply be too late. The earth will not be able to sustain human life. We only have a few years—five at the most—to turn this around before it is too late!"

I know that the changes in the environment caused by human disregard for the planet and other living beings are devastating and enormous. I can see it in my own communities' concern for things as fundamental to life as safe drinking water and breathable air. I believe her predictions are based on her sincere assessment of the information she has, although I have no way of judging the accuracy of her time line. But I also know that her sense of urgency, even if her predictions are accurate, will not get her the result she seeks. I can feel within myself and throughout the audience resistance to her certainty that we are out of time. If we buy it, if we follow and identify exclusively with the fear stirred by her words, we will become either paralyzed by the magnitude of what needs to be done or galvanized into endless, exhausting, and not necessarily effective doing, driven by a desperate desire to change what is. The latter is something I have experienced all too often. The fruits of that labor are scant, and the cost, the depletion of inner resources consumed at the high rate of fear, sooner or later brings collapse.

I cannot help but wonder what would happen if Janice let herself sink down into the feeling she is trying to outrun, if she just sat with her certainty that human beings will not do what is necessary and will destroy this planet's ability to sustain us. What if she simply stayed with the fear and anger and grief that this must stir in her?

I am not judging Janice for wanting to outrun these feelings, for wanting to do what she thinks will create community action she believes is imperative if we are to stave off impending global devastation. I can't sit still with my feelings of panic when I spill a half-cup of tea on my laptop keyboard, seemingly destroying the hard drive and the nearly completed manuscript it holds! I fly into frantic doing, phoning anyone I can think of who might know of some miraculous way to undo the damage, driving through a blinding snowstorm for two hours to take the computer to a repair shop, searching frantically for the backup disks I think I made just before our recent move to a new home. How much harder to be with our thoughts and feelings when it seems that the future of the world is at stake?

What happens when the situation is dire, when we are certain that unless something is done, serious consequences will result? Surely that's a time to set aside spiritual not-doing, to roll up our sleeves and get to it. Surely there are some situations in which we have to just do it!

No. Because it doesn't work.

Choices that are determined by fear are unlikely to be wise ones. Doing that requires endless effort—and all doing, because it is a pulling away from what is, requires an infinite supply of new energy—is not sustainable. Choices that come from being with what is no matter how dire or immediate will come with greater ease, cost less energy, and be more effective in recreating the balance from which they come. There can be no separation between means and ends. We cannot create a personal life or a world economy that is sustainable by being dedicated to what is inherently not sustainable—doing.

What would it have looked like if I had been able to just be with my tea-soaked computer and my frantic feelings? Would I still have called someone for advice, taken it to a repair shop, looked for the backup disks? Probably, although had I sat down and waited until, as Lao Tzu says, my "mud settled," I probably would have waited until the driving conditions improved, not risking life and limb in the process. More important, my experience would have been very different. I probably would have made the trip into the city less frenetically, might even have enjoyed it, and I probably would not have been so exhausted at the end of it all. I might even, with a calm, clear mind, have remembered where the backup disks were without searching. Certainly I would not have suffered as much, worrying that the computer was irreparable, the information irretrievable, and the backup disks lost forever in the chaos of moving.

Would Janice still work to bring about a sustainable way of living on the earth if she were able to sit still with both the information she has and the feelings they raise? I don't know, but I am guessing she would. I do not doubt her love for the earth. But I cannot help but imagine that her voice might be more easily and completely heard if it flowed from and was full of that love and grief, instead of the frantic fear that we will not do enough fast enough.

Sometimes the movement that flows from not-doing looks similar to the doing dictated by fear and shaped by the burning desire to change what is. But the quality of the action, the taste of the experience, and subsequently the consequences that flow from this movement are very different.

When I clean my house because it is one more thing on my long list of things to be done, a job I want out of the way, I am rarely in the present moment with my task. Tidying a room because I cannot stand the mess and fear that it will gradually take over and bury me, I tire easily but refuse to stop and rest. I am focused on the goal of finishing the task. I want what is—the mess—to be changed. The quality of my movement and my experience is very different when I let the impulse to care for my home, to create beauty and comfort, pull me into mopping the floor or doing the dishes or tidying up a room with a conscious connection to an inner stillness. I am more likely to take on smaller pieces of the work and enjoy the process, moving more slowly and stopping after even a small bit has been accomplished to rest or move in another direction.

Observing over time these two ways of moving in even the simplest of tasks, I discover to my surprise that I do not necessarily accomplish more by doing, and even when I do, the pleasure I receive from the increased achievement is so small and so temporary that it does not balance out the resulting tiredness and lost moments or hours when I am not present but missing my own life and the joy it can bring. Not only that, but the quality of my movement affects those around me. Doing, I am more likely to be irritable and resentful of those I feel are not doing as much, and they are understandably more likely to avoid me and resist participating in what feels like endless work.

Houses that are lived in get messy and dirty over and over again. People who are attacked and hurt or have had someone close to them attacked and hurt, as was true for so many on September 11, become frightened and angry, often wanting to strike out against those they think are responsible. And Janice is correct: current technologies and lifestyles in the West are depleting or destroying vast quantities of natural resources needed to sustain life on this planet. This is what is. But if we could simply be with these and the infinite other things that simply are, a different way of taking care of ourselves and our world might arise from deep within us. Maybe the house does not need to be as neat and clean as once seemed imperative, or the tasks at hand can be done with an appreciation for the joy of having a home to care for, in a way that does not exhaust or seem burdensome. Maybe there are ways to express our grief at violence and injustice other than striking back, ways that will not only release the anguish in our own hearts but also begin to heal the heart of a world divided by injustice and the illusion of different and separate self-interests. Maybe being fully with the current reality of environmental destruction and the feelings this raises can lead us back into a relationship with the earth that sustains us and all others living on this planet, into a relationship that would simply make polluting, resource-depleting technologies unprofitable because no one would feel drawn to use them.

And I think of my own life and the choices I have. Maybe I can offer as much if I visit and speak with three or four groups a year rather than saying yes to all invitations, spurred on by warnings from well-meaning friends and colleagues that I must "strike while the iron is hot," take advantage of all opportunities if I am to have the book sales and income that allow me to continue to do what I love. Maybe I can offer more to those I am with if I am not so tired, if I leave room to embody more consistently the stillness I talk about instead of hoping to touch a moment of full awareness during my morning practice before I head off to do what I or others think is required. Maybe it doesn't matter if I always and exclusively get to do what I love if I can more consistently love and find joy in wherever I am by allowing each movement—whether washing the floor, writing a book, or speaking to a group—to come from a deep and sacred spaciousness within.

I am reminded of a story from my childhood, of Jesus asking his disciples to look at the lilies of the field and consider how beautiful they are despite the fact that they do not work, do not do anything. What a strange mystery it is, this conviction we hold that we must continuously do in order to stave off disaster! In so doing we often create the very suffering we hope to avoid. Convinced by our culture and our fear that we are what we do, we move too quickly, too soon, and too incessantly to let the purpose of our existence, the meaning in the very essence of what we are, shape our lives.

Meditation on Stopping

Just before my forty-day retreat, racing through a particularly busy day of tracking down and buying supplies for my trek into the wilderness, where I hoped to slow down and be present, I came up with a mantra. This was a surprise, given my misgivings about the ways in which mantras are misused to escape, avoid, or deny what is in the present moment. But in the midst of rushing around to get ready for being present somewhere else at sometime in the future, I said to myself over and over, no matter what I was doing, no matter how imperative speeding up seemed to be:

"I will not allow anyone or anything to make me rush."

Try it for one day. Pick a busy day, just say it to yourself periodically, and watch how often you catch yourself rushing. Rushing, by definition, means you are not in the present moment, are anticipating catching the elevator, getting through that amber light, finishing some project before a real or imagined deadline.

I realize that the unusual thing about this mantra is that it's negative, but that's what worked for me. I could have said, "I will slow down and savor the moment," but I know myself well enough to know that I could say this, could add one more thing to the long list of what I think I should be doing, while still moving at high speed, anticipating getting ahead of the throng at the traffic light or zipping into the bank just before it closes for the day. This is a mantra for not-doing, for stopping one thing—rushing.

Nine

The God-Mad

⸎

Let yourself be one of the God-mad,
faithful only to the Beauty you are.

I should tell you from the start that I've been having a difficult time with this chapter, writing and discarding pages,
moving on to complete or rewrite other parts of the book.
The other chapters are complete, but still this one cries out to me,
tells me that I am hedging, not allowing the truth to speak to me or
you about what it means to be God-mad. So I begin again. It's not
that I don't understand this small segment of the prose poem or
that I disagree with its directive to allow my experience of what is
both the essence of what I am and larger than myself to determine
my actions regardless of what others will think. It's that I find my
life woefully lacking in instances when I have allowed myself to
follow unreservedly the impulse that comes from the moment of
fully and ecstatically touching the beauty of the divine within and
around me.

Of course I do have my private moments of letting my intimacy with the Beloved have its uncensored way with me.

Years ago, I often drove alone to a small trailer I owned on an isolated wilderness campsite, arriving late at night. Each time I arrived I would step from the car after turning off my headlights and shout exuberantly into the welcoming darkness, "Hi, honey, I'm home!" listening to my voice echo across the lake to the unmoving silhouettes of hemlocks and white pines on the opposite shore and up through the air to infinite points of light in an indigo sky. This earth, this universe, this breathtaking manifestation of the divine presence, is the home I love, and nowhere do I feel this more strongly than when I am in the Canadian wilderness. The beauty of this place and my sheer delight at being there made the words spill out of me, unconcerned about how crazy most people would probably think it was to call out to the trees and sky and rocks and water as if I were coming home and greeting an intimately familiar partner. Because I was.

Of course, I also knew that no one—no other person—could hear me. Like most people, I behave, even without thinking, according to commonly agreed on social norms, which don't include calling out to the trees and sky and rocks and water. Some might think that I've already pushed that envelope by using the name Oriah Mountain Dreamer. In fact, I can't even claim using the name as a courageous act defying social convention. I was given the name by one of the Native American elders with whom I studied, and initially I never used it outside the context of sacred ceremony. But because the prose poem "The Invitation" had been offered first to students who knew me in the context of ceremony as Oriah Mountain Dreamer, the name went with the poem when it was passed around the world. Although program directors, TV producers, and interviewers often complain that the name is problematic, that it makes others suspicious that I may be a little crazy or flaky (a sentiment I completely understand and would probably share if approached by someone else with this name), the name has stuck. When I'm interviewed, one of the first questions I am most often asked is, "That's not your *real* name, is it?"

To which I lightly respond, "Oh, it's a real name all right. It's just not my birth name." Historically, in many cultures a name taken as part of a spiritual path is considered far more real than one given at birth, when so little is known about the character or future of the individual. But reality is culturally defined, and in my culture the names deemed real are the names that reflect the husband or father to whom you belong and from whom you are entitled to inherit property, because blood ties and property are generally accepted as considerably more real than spiritual experiences.

So I have resigned myself to being known as Oriah Mountain Dreamer and dealing with the reactions this causes, laughing along with hotel personnel who stumble over "Yes, Ms. Mountain . . . um . . . I mean, Ms. Dreamer . . ." when confirming my room service order. This resignation could hardly be touted as an instance of defiant faithfulness to my deepest essence or spiritual experience.

Craziness is commonly understood to be an unwillingness or inability to participate in the cultural agreements we make about what is real—that to which we collectively attribute not only existence but also meaning and importance. I do not want to make light of the suffering endured when someone afflicted with mental illness cannot determine any qualitative difference between the voice of the person in front of them saying hello and the voice in their mind's ear telling them to hide in the basement because someone is coming to harm them tonight. When I was employed as a social worker I found that the line between neuroses we all share and psychosis, which is fortunately less common, was generally and sadly very clear when you were in a room with someone suffering the latter.

The ability to understand and take into account how your culture defines reality is one sign of being grounded, sane. But what happens when your experiences lie outside this culturally acceptable definition of reality, as many spiritual experiences do? Surely Moses paused and wondered if he was losing his mind when he heard a burning bush speak to him. Do Christians who believe in the virgin birth think Mary's friends and family believed her when she turned up pregnant and said she had never had sex? What reaction do you think Jesus' disciples got when they went home and reported feeding hundreds with only a few loaves of bread and a small number of fish? History is full of stories of those we revere as great saints or teachers, thought by many during their time to be simply mad. One of my favorites is the story of Mirabai, the sixteenth-century Indian mystic and poet. Mirabai was a devotee of the Hindu God Shiva. Widowed at an early age and refusing to follow the cultural norm and throw herself on her husband's funeral pyre, Mirabai gave up her jewels and silk dresses to wander the countryside singing and dancing and reciting poetry in praise of God. Her in-laws were so furious they tried to have her killed to stop her craziness and the shame they felt it brought upon them.

What would it look like if we allowed ourselves to be God-mad, if we simply decided to stop whatever we were doing and wait until the impulse to move came from a deep awareness of the sacred presence within and around us and then followed wherever it led? When I think of this happening in the world I imagine a work-weary woman in a busy office suddenly pausing at her desk, doing nothing for a moment, and then getting up and quietly walking out the door, leaving her computer running and her co-workers baffled. I imagine a man sitting in his living room, dozing in front of the TV as he does every night after dinner, suddenly turning his head as if to catch the echo of some sound coming to him from a great distance and after listening for a minute, getting up and, without bothering to turn off the TV, walking outside and continuing in the direction of the setting sun.

Oh, I know what you're thinking: How will the woman pay her bills without her job? What about that man's responsibilities to his family? But you're leaping to conclusions about what will happen next. Maybe the woman finds another way to provide for herself and her family that does not rob her soul of the joy she longs for every day. Maybe she finds she does not need as much, or maybe she returns tomorrow and finds a different way to be in that office. Maybe the man, waking up from his habitual patterns and walking toward what calls him, really sees his family for the first time and can offer them something more than the tired absence of daily routines divorced from the meaning at the center of his life.

I am not suggesting that listening to the call will necessarily require that you leave your job or turn off your TV, although I admit

I could launch a pretty good argument for the latter. One person may be able to be faithful to the beauty of being aware of his or her essential nature, to the ecstasy of touching the Beloved daily, and still work in an office, while another may need to leave. The hard part is that we cannot predict what the call will require, how that sacred stillness at the center of all that is might inspire us to move if we have the courage to simply sit with it and follow the impulse to move when it comes.

I know that what I am talking about here, the not-doing that allows something other than the desire to change things guide our movements, is by current cultural standards crazy. If you doubt this, consider where it might lead. How much of what we do might be left undone if we truly sat with and waited for the impulse to move to find us from deep within the presence that surrounds and sustains us? Would anyone feel drawn to start another war or diligently pursue a career that did not bring real joy to themselves or beauty to the world? Would anyone spontaneously find in that great well of silence the overwhelming impulse to invent yet another shade of lipstick, another gas-guzzling automobile, another fridge magnet or innovative product like pet rocks? Maybe some things just wouldn't get done, and what might that mean to our way of life? What if, in realizing how precious our awareness of the Beloved is, in tasting the joy that flows from being present, we simply insisted that we would move only as fast and only in the direction we could move without losing the exquisite taste of that which is larger and yet within each of us? Many around you would think you mad, particularly if the impulse you followed involved turning away even temporarily from what this culture promotes as most real and most valuable. Yes, I mean if your movement took you in a direction that cut into income or profits.

So, at the risk of leaving you shaking your head in dismay, let me tell you about one time when I can truly say I allowed myself to be God-mad, to follow the impulse that came from deep within my essential self even when it cost me something that those around me considered valuable. I don't expect you to approve. I have discovered that no matter how much those who are interested in cultivating a spiritual life are drawn to and admire the *idea* of being God-mad, when our choices run contrary to the social values we breathe in daily, they stir fear and anger.

I am about to go on the road for a second book tour. I have accepted invitations to speak at a variety of venues. While I'm looking forward to meeting the different groups, I also have some trepidation, aware that on my first book tour I had at best an intermittent awareness of any internal stillness as I traveled. Some of this was simply adapting to the unfamiliarity of frequent traveling, hotel living, and meeting so many new people. As much as I appreciate room service—and I *really* do appreciate it—there can be something a little ungrounding, a little unreal, about returning to your room to discover all your mess has disappeared as if by magic, particularly when you are used to doing all of your own cleaning up. But the real challenge was to remember why I wrote in the first place when enthusiastic publicists, conference promoters, and program directors were offering what they felt was helpful advice and encouragement on how to take full advantage of good book sales to increase my income and profile.

Now, I have nothing against making money, and I know that personal appearances help to make a book available to readers. I felt like I had been not so much drawn into the pursuit of fame and fortune as thrown too often off center by being surrounded by the noises of that pursuit. Perhaps this is in part because I am Canadian. Canada has the same kind of economic system and materialist values as the United States. The difference is volume. Since Canada has only one-tenth the population spread over an enormous expanse of land, Canadians simply do not have the same number of opportunities at home to make substantial sums of money. Never mind that most Americans and Canadians never make millions, the siren song of the possibility is much louder in the States. Canadians are not more virtuous about making money—although it is possible that the less extroverted culture in Canada covets fame less—they simply don't have the same level of temptation or opportunity to make it an exclusive or superseding goal.

I am spending a lot of time in prayer preparing for my second book tour, asking for a way to stay centered and unattached to the subtle and not-so-subtle pressures to make decisions about my future based on what seems likely to increase income. I am trying to find my way into not-doing, into not allowing my thoughts or others' evaluations about which venues would give the greatest monetary return to determine my actions.

In addition to these inner concerns, I have gone to an immigration lawyer to get the proper papers for working in the United States. According to the lawyer and others I know doing similar work in the States, the work I am about to do fits neatly into one of the categories in the North American Free Trade Agreement that allows people in certain occupations from both sides of the border to work in either country. Armed with all the proper paperwork, my friend Linda and I decide to drive down to Buffalo one weekend to acquire the visa while visiting some local theaters nearby on the Canadian side. Much to our shock, when I arrive at the border and my papers are examined, the man in charge tells me in no uncertain terms that I do not fit the visa category, will not be allowed to cross the border on that day, and will be watched carefully in the future.

I am stunned. I have made commitments to over a dozen upcoming events, ensuring an income of about sixty thousand American dollars over the next year, money that will support my sons and me for at least the next eighteen months, even after the 50 percent tax rate in Canada takes its toll. Although we can manage on saved book royalties, I am concerned about not fulfilling the commitments I have made and worried about prospects for making necessary future income. I wake up in the middle of the night feeling sick with anxiety, trying to find a solution. Unable to get back to sleep, I get up and begin to do my practice of prayer and meditation, sitting in the dark on the floor at the foot of my bed. As I sit and focus on my breath, I call out to the Grandmothers, the old women I have often seen in my night dreams and meditations. "Help me," I whisper into the dim light. "I don't know what to do." Slowly I begin to relax. As the chatter of mental problem solving drifts away I become still, aware of my body and the room, filled at last with a deep sense of spaciousness, watching my thoughts and feelings drift by.

"What do you want most?" a voice inside me asks quietly.

My answer comes immediately from the clear quiet within. "To stay centered in what I am, in my connection to the Sacred Mystery, to cross the border without any anxiety."

"Then don't take the money. If you don't take the money you don't have to worry about it at all."

Right away I know this is the solution, not only to the immediate problem of crossing the border without lying or hedging on the truth, but also to my quest to find a way to stay clear of the temptation to let my own or others' attachment to or fear about money muddy my process of choosing where I will go or what I can offer at different venues. I feel a rush of almost giddy gratitude for the clarity that has arisen so easily when I managed to stop struggling to find a solution with my mind.

As I sit with the idea of not receiving the speaking fees, remembering how tiring some of the touring was after the first book, I wonder to myself, "If I'm not being paid, will I travel and speak at all?"

The voice of the Grandmother that comes holds just a hint of laughter. Apparently my choices, as I suspected, have not been entirely free from the desire for monetary gain. "Well, I guess that depends on whether or not you have anything you want to say and if these are the people you want to say it to."

Considering this, I find that I do want to talk with people, want to share with them in person the ideas and experiences I write about. So I am clear: I will do the speaking that has been arranged, but beyond covering expenses I will not accept any fee. I know I cannot do this indefinitely but also know that the royalty payments will take care of my family for the next year. Wondering how far into the unknown and unpredictable future I need to be able to extend the illusion of control by amassing savings, I decide that at the moment, knowing we are okay for the next year is just fine.

When I get home I call Anna, the organizer of the first conference at which I am scheduled to speak, and tell her what has happened. Since she is committed to developing and sharing the spiritual aspect of life, I tell her about my relief at finding a way to be with people, free of the motivation or need to make money. I ask her to send my speaking fee to Mark Kelso, the talented composer and musician who has offered at his own expense to accompanying me at this conference when I recite poetry. There is a long, strange pause, silence from the other end of the phone.

Finally Anna speaks, blurting out, "Well, we're planning to get a lot more meticulous in our bookkeeping and income reporting than we have been!" Her voice is defensive, almost hostile.

I don't know what to say. Clearly Anna has taken my choice to be an indictment of her own financial practices, something I know and care nothing about. I try again to explain that this choice, although necessitated by the border official's decision, is one that helps me step aside from monetary concerns and focus on the deeper reasons for attending events like her conference. Hoping to sound more sane, I assure her that I will not be able to do this indefinitely, will have to make money in the future to support myself and my sons. I can tell that my explanations are doing little to reassure her that I am not simply crazy.

In a prosperous, materialist culture, even among those who are committed to and focused on developing and living by values consistent with and shaped by their spirituality, there is little you can do that will seem crazier than turning down money. One woman, an old and dear friend who is a longtime yoga teacher and practitioner, tells me with great vehemence, "You can't do this! You can't refuse the money. It's your work, so it's your money. You have to take it!"

I am mystified by the strength of her response and point out that if it is my money then I can do anything I want, including refusing to accept it.

"If you were coming from the right place, from a deep spiritual clarity, you would be able to take the money or leave the money and not have it affect your choices or the way you are with people either way," she points out fiercely.

I laugh. "You're absolutely right," I tell her, "but I think I probably have to practice not taking the money before I can claim to know that I could take it or leave it."

A week after I get home from the border visit the immigration lawyer calls to say he has worked out the misunderstanding with the American officials and my visa will be waiting for me at the airport. For half a second I wonder, "Now what?" but my choice has been made. The provision of the visa simply means that I do not have to share my decision with all the program directors and conference organizers I am working with and so do not have to deal with their reactions to my decision. I don't want to evangelize, I simply want to do what I know will allow me at this time to learn more about staying connected to my sense of the Beloved within and around me. So, visa in hand, I accept the speaking fees and simply pass the money along, sometimes to Mark, sometimes to a friend in need, sometimes to a poet who has touched my heart with his or her words.

You know you've touched a core belief of a culture when you do something contrary to its dictates that does absolutely no harm and you are met with incredulous looks and vehement protests. To be God-mad is to be willing to follow the knowing that comes from deep within your essential nature, from your awareness of that which is larger than yourself, even when you cannot justify your choices to those around you.

Today, wondering at my own resistance to writing this chapter, I sit and contemplate what it would look like for me to be God-mad, for me to follow the movement that springs from my experience of the sacred life force within and around me, right now. And I see an image of myself handing out copies of poems, ecstatic poems about experiencing the Beloved, to all those who pass a busy street corner in Toronto's financial district. The image makes me laugh. To hand out copies of poems by Rumi and Hafiz and Mirabai, by Meister Eckhart and St. Francis and Teresa of Avila, to offer them to anyone who passes, not asking for or advertising anything but simply sharing the beauty of words written by those who experienced the freedom of knowing that to which they belong— what gloriously subversive mischief! It reminds me of something Daniel Ladinsky, the translator of these and many other great poets, wrote to me last week. During an e-mail discussion about doing a recording of these poems, Daniel said that he thought of sharing these poems as sending "medics into the field." And I think, "Yes!"

Being God-mad is being willing to find your way of making love to the world today. I think of Rumi's words as Coleman Barks has translated them in *Rumi: The Book of Love:*

Remember, the way you make love is the way God will be with you.

And I remember watching Mother Teresa in a film made by my dear friend Ann Petrie, feeling the love this tiny nun had for those she sought to comfort. Her tireless ability to offer care to the poorest of the poor was fueled by her ability to see in the person lying in the street her Beloved—Jesus—incarnate. She touched the world and those in need as any of us would touch the one with whom we are in love, with passion and tenderness.

Years ago I had a dream in which I was standing in front of the Grandmothers with a group of women who had studied and participated in ceremony and meditation with me. There was a sense of formality in the meeting between these two groups. One of the Grandmothers spoke and asked, "Who are you?"

And I replied, "We are the women who make love to the world to take the war out of it."

Now, many years later, I realize that I cannot take the war out of the world unless I can stop my own daily war with reality, my own fight with what is within and around me. And stopping this war, making love to the world, means making a commitment to following the movement that arises from the deep stillness this acceptance allows, even when others may think my choices are crazy. After all, doesn't all great lovemaking, the kind that takes your breath away with the fire of its passion and the beauty of its tenderness, require letting go of worrying about how you look or what the neighbors may think when they hear you moaning in ecstasy? To make love passionately to the world or another, you have to be fully present to the only moment you have, this one right now. You have to learn to see without judgment the one to whom you make love—the human man or woman you touch, yourself as you are right now, and this world today just as it is—accurately and compassionately. And you have to be willing to surrender to the heat that can carry you into a deeper union, to the awareness that is beyond thought, to the being at the center of what you are, letting your essence shape how you touch and respond to being touched.

I could say more about making love to the world, but I have to go now and make copies of some poems I know and love.

Meditation on Being God-Mad

Do this meditation in the spirit of exploration. I find it easiest when trying to uncover new information about reality—inner or outer—to have a pen and paper handy. Writing allows me to sidestep the judging, censoring voice within, to discover something I don't already know. You may want to write what comes, or, if you find writing is for you an impediment to allowing the flow of whatever comes, set it aside and allow the answers to simply arise in your consciousness.

Sit in a comfortable position. Take three deep breaths and let your shoulders drop. With each exhale allow yourself to let all expectations and fears float gently away. What we are doing here is simply opening to what is already there within you. You are not required to *do* anything. Let your body relax, and with each exhale allow any tiredness or tension to float away. If you find yourself thinking about what might or might not happen, what you want to or are afraid will happen, simply acknowledge the thoughts and let them move through you, gently bringing your attention back to your breath.

Allow the following questions or phrases to come into your mind, waiting in silence for a while between them for whatever comes. Notice, without any judgment, the answers or the completion of the phrases that come. Notice any thoughts or feelings you have about what comes. Do some excite or entice? Do others frighten or intimidate? Let the feelings move through you, and bring your attention back to your breath, focusing on one or two inhales and exhales before you move on to the next question or phrase.

What would it look like today to be God-mad?

What would it look like to let my longing for the Beloved spill into every moment of this day?

If it didn't seem so crazy I'd . . .

How do I want God (the Mystery, the Beloved, the Great Mother . . .) to be with me?

Given this, how do I want to make love to the world today?

Ten

Lost

Let the Lover pull you to your feet and hold you close,
dancing even when fear urges you to sit this one out.

*I*n some ways, experiencing the deep peace of being awake
to what you are and then losing connection with this
awareness, feeling unable to wake up instantly, can be
more painful than when you were unconscious.

The feeling in my body when I slip away from being present,
when I fall out of my awareness of being into doing, reminds me of
dreams I had when my children were very young. In my exhaustion and my anxiety about being an adequate mother, I would
dream that I had forgotten one of my sons in a store or another
public place. Terrified that he would be harmed, I would tell myself, "It's only a dream. It's not real. Just wake up!" and I would
open my eyes and find myself in my bed, my heart pounding in
my ears. But no sooner had I started to calm down when some
bizarre incident—like a creeping paralysis in my limbs as I tried to
go to a screaming son being carried from the house by a maraud-
ing intruder—would let me know that I was still sleeping and

dreaming, and I would once again struggle to wake up. Some nights this exhausting and desperate bid to wake up would repeat over and over again.

Sometimes this is what it is like to live for even a moment in the center of your awareness of what you are and then to lose this awareness. You know you are asleep, but you just cannot wake up. When we have become wholly identified with passing thoughts and feelings, usually strong and often painful thoughts and feelings that seem to overwhelm and define who we are in this moment, we cannot find our ability to sit within the still center of simply being. In these moments we feel that the still center is an inaccessible fantasy. We become certain that we simply can't get there from here. We may not even want to be present in these moments, may feel like we want out of our own skin. But if we have had an experience of our essential nature, of sitting in the now fully, we may remember that this too shall pass and may be able to observe how this loss of consciousness happens.

I cringe a little to tell my stories of failing to stay awake. Our wounds and our fears are more common than unique, more humbling than enlightening or entertaining. Your stories of fear overwhelming your awareness of all that you are will be different in the details but the same in their essence. I share these stories because I want to know and share how it is that a woman who knows what she is, who has experienced her inner essence and the deep peace this presence brings, can lose this sense completely and then find her way back to it again and again. Because this is what it is sometimes like to be human: to be so awake you cannot imagine ever going back to sleep again, and then to be lost in a nightmare from which you feel you simply cannot awaken. I am interested in finding ways to alleviate suffering in myself and in the world, so the stories of how we discover a way out of the darkness of separation and suffering interest me as much as the stories of grace-given peace.

I am unpacking boxes of files and books in my new office and writing studio. It is late. I cannot see out into the blackness beyond the windows, but I can hear the wind blowing the deep snow into high-peaked drifts around our new home. A recording, a gift from the staff at Sounds True Audio I received months ago, entitled *The Scent of Light,* plays on the CD player that has finally been unpacked and hooked up in the corner. Accompanied by the plaintive wail of the sitar, a man's voice slowly recites the ecstatically inspired poems of Hafiz, the fourteenth-century Sufi mystic, as they have been translated by Daniel Ladinsky. But the words roll off me like raindrops hitting canvas. They do not penetrate my gloom. I am tired, moving mechanically after too many days of planning and packing and painting. My back aches from lifting boxes, and I have no strength in my left arm from overextending my elbow at some point in the process of moving. Only four months ago I had had whole days of acting from deep stillness, but the last four weeks have been a blur of frantic doing. Concerned about moving a household and business when all I really want to do is write, pressed by the seemingly endless details of moving right after our wedding celebration and in the midst of Christmas holiday preparations, I have lost all sense of not-doing. All my movements have turned into a relentless quest to have everything settled in the new home so I can resume writing by the first week of January. Focused on this goal and fueled by my anxiety that it will not be accomplished, I move through

tasks with undaunted perseverance but little joy, pushing and prod-
ding and dragging the men I love, my two sons and Jeff, along with
me, pressing them to work steadily from early morning until we all
drop exhausted into our beds late at night.

The thing that is so discouraging is that I have been able to see it
happening, have never really lost sight of what I was doing, have remained conscious enough to see myself frantically running and yet
still been unable or unwilling—I cannot tell which—to stop. I have
failed the "test" I saw before me only six weeks earlier. I did not trust
my deep inner stillness to guide me in getting done what was needed
and so took over with all my ego strength and pushed through. In
doing so, I know that I have lost access to the wisdom that might
have guided me in knowing what really does need to be done and
what could wait or be let go. When I am caught in drivenness, only
perfection will do, all tasks appear critical, and failure to meet anxi-
ety-ridden and ever-rising expectations promises unspecified disaster.

How can I write about heeding the call to stop doing, to simply be and let all movement come from the place of stillness, when
I am so caught up in doing? Is not-doing possible only if we have
no deadlines, no obligations, when we are feeling calm and centered? If so, it's not much good in a human life. But the truth is, I
had a choice. I could see what was happening, and I chose doing,
chose to keep going. Somewhere deep inside I told myself I would
go back to not-doing, back to cultivating my awareness of inner
stillness, once the boxes were unpacked, after all the painting was
complete and the tasks were caught up. I know this is crazy. The
tasks around a home are never finished, and a spiritual practice

that cannot be maintained in the midst of life, particularly when things are stressful, is not useful for connecting with ourselves or that which is larger than ourselves.

I am overwhelmed by feelings of failure, by my sense of having betrayed the Sacred Mystery, that which has given me an exquisite taste of my essential nature. But still, knowing that I need to stop but feeling frozen in my misery, I continue to unpack boxes, sure in some dark corner of my heart that I will be deservedly abandoned by the Beloved that calls my name for not heeding the call, for seeing what is needed and simply not having whatever it takes to stop. I accept my failure with a kind of dismal stoicism, muttering bleakly and repeatedly to myself as I empty and flatten another box, "You are not handling this well."

Suddenly I am aware of the words to the poem that is being spoken on the CD player. Unexpected, they stop me where I stand. I listen and feel an unforeseen thawing of my body and heart that allows me to feel in places where I have had only a sense of being frozen, numb. I go down on my knees there in the middle of packing materials and boxes. Something inside loosens, and tears begin to flow as Hafiz's words touch me gently, splitting me open.

You have
not danced so badly, my dear,
trying to hold hands with the Beautiful One,

You have waltzed with great style my sweet, crushed angel,
to have even neared God's heart at all.

Our Partner is notoriously hard to follow, and even His
best musicians are not always easy to hear.

So what, if the music has stopped for a while.
So what, if the price of admission to the Divine is out of reach
   tonight.

So what my sweetheart, if you lack the ante to gamble for real love.

The mind and the body are famous for holding the heart ransom,
but Hafiz knows the Beloved's eternal habits. Have patience,
for He will not be able to resist your longings
and charms for long.

You have not danced so badly, my dear,
trying to kiss the Magnificent
One.

You have actually waltzed with tremendous style,
my sweet, O my sweet,
crushed
angel.

One of the difficulties of knowing what you are and why you
are here and then losing and regaining that awareness is the temptation to identify with feelings of shame for failing to hold close to
you what you know. But never, in all my experiences of the presence that I am or of that greater mystery in which I participate,

have I ever caught even a glimpse of judgment or recrimination. Shame only makes it harder to be with what is. Pulling away from what is, even when what is is being disconnected from the experience of our essence, is continuing the war with reality. We cannot end this war by doing but only by following our longing, letting it lead us back into simply being.

I have great faith in our longing as a portal that can take us to what we are if we follow it down into the deepest ache of the soul. But longing—the ache for something more than just continuing—is not the same as craving. Craving is fueled by fear and pushes for speed and doing, whereas longing wants to linger with, go deeper into, and learn from what is in the present moment. Craving is never really satisfied, is always reaching for more, looking to some other time and place, to the idealized past or hoped-for future satisfaction. Craving most often focuses on the particular form of what we want: a particular relationship, a specific job, a certain kind of home or some other possession—even spiritual fulfillment. Longing will take us to the knowledge of our essence and the meaning enfolded in being what we are.

Longing and craving can, at least initially, look alike, but they lead down very different roads. Sometimes, when the heat of my battle with reality is at its height, when I am certain that my very existence depends upon changing what I see as unjust or simply wrong—whether an attitude or feeling within myself or a circumstance in the world—when I am caught in craving, attached to the outcome of my actions and disconnected from my deeper longing, I mistake the call, the tug that pulls at my weary heart, for an admonishment to fight more fiercely, to try harder. And I become not called but driven. Filled with what may look to others like the passion of sincere conviction, I resolve to do whatever I imagine it will take—to follow the longing impeccably, to live what matters consistently, to allow the complete unfolding of who I am—so well, so perfectly, that I will transform aspects of my personality, will be forever changed into a kinder, gentler Oriah.

When we are driven we don't want to end the war, we want to win it.

I wish I could tell you that the minute I was broken open by the words of Hafiz's poem, I stopped doing and sat in the center of my essential stillness. But as Hafiz wrote, some nights you simply don't have the price of admission to touch the divine. What a challenge this is for a perfectionist—to face that at moments I simply cannot find what it takes to be consciously aware! All my life I have warred with this reality, pressing myself to pull more resources from a deeper place, to try harder, do better. And Hafiz says, "So what if you can't right now! Relax." This is not a giving up but a giving over to what is true in the present moment.

And the moment I accept what is, something begins to shift within me. Over the next few days I begin to sit, not with the still center of my essence, but with my anxiety, my fear of being abandoned by the Beloved because I could not maintain my awareness of who I am and why I am here. And as I do so, my longing to stop and simply be—the longing Hafiz assures me the Beloved cannot resist for long—grows larger than my fear of not getting things done on time.

If we can see our doing, if we are conscious of moving when we need to sit still, aware that we have fallen from following the flow into relentlessly pushing the river, and yet continue to do, usually we will find we are fighting something in the current reality, something we are trying to overcome or outrun, something we are hoping will change before we have to look it directly in the face. The good news is that one moment of conscious stopping will often lead to another, and then another and another.

I keep working, but I slow down a little and watch myself. And I become aware of a level of turmoil within that surpasses my fear that the unpacking will not be done in time for me to resume writing in January. There is a shakiness, a kind of confusion, a strange mix of feelings of bewilderment and grief in the center of my body and heart. There is . . . an emptiness I do not understand. It takes a few days, but eventually I simply sit with and begin to understand what has been unfamiliar and frightening.

I am reminded of all the change that has happened in my life over the last three years. All that I identified as myself—the roles I have played in my home and my community, my primary relationships, and the nature of my work—has changed. If I were writing a novel about a woman based on my own life three years ago, she would be a single mother of two teenage sons living in socialized housing. She would live in the center of a large city, inundated by the noise of streetcars and close neighbors playing pianos, stereos, and saxophones too late at night and the sound of trucks backing up, construction workers shouting, and dogs barking too early in the morning. She would be frugal, careful with money, accustomed to having very little but comfortable with making do. Unexpected expenses, like a punctured radiator in her twelve-year-old car, would require creative thinking and fortuitous blessings like scrap yard finds and unexpected gifts. Her work involves counseling individuals and sharing the spiritual teachings and practices she has learned over fifteen years with small groups in workshops, evening classes, and week-long retreats. She has built and maintains an intimate community, primarily of women and including a few close friends, by helping people connect to themselves and each other in the context of shared ceremony, self-examination, and prayer. Between the daily mothering of two sons, giving to and receiving support and assistance from friends, and maintaining the community of students who study with her, her life is full of people and responsibilities and the daily drama these bring.

If I were writing a story based on my life today, the woman would look very different. She would be married and living with her husband in a modest but beautiful home in the country, surrounded by the deep silence of a large forest. Deer come to drink at the pond outside her door, and the echo of the coyotes' howl is the only sound that breaks the night stillness. Her sons, young men in their early twenties, visit occasionally on weekends when their studies and their jobs in the city two hours away allow them to make the trip. Her work is solitary, writing alone in the quiet of her home and traveling occasionally to speak with crowds of friendly strangers in groups as large as two thousand. Her books are selling, the invitations to speak continue, and her husband is employed, so even with two sons in university there is enough money so that unexpected expenses do not cause lost sleep or necessitate material sacrifices. She is new to the area where she is living and so knows no one, has no tight-knit community with whom she shares a history. Most of the locals are farmers, many devoted Mennonites who have lived in the area for generations. Her life intersects with theirs primarily around tasks like snow removal or wood delivery, and there are few opportunities to get to know these polite, friendly people.

I know what you're thinking: what's the problem? The changes are good. The surprise, which leaves a strange hollow feeling in the center of my body, is that I was and still am to some degree identified with the woman in the first story. That's who I was for over sixteen years, and all that is gone. The new is wonderful but . . . it is new. I have not yet identified with the married woman living quietly and comfortably close to the land. It doesn't feel like me. As I realize this, I am shocked to see how much of what I do is determined by a set of beliefs I have about what is required in certain roles. My beliefs may not correspond to ones held by the mainstream culture—in fact in some instances have probably been shaped by a deliberate if somewhat unconscious desire to reject mainstream cultural expectations—but they still offer a kind of conceptual prepackaging of life. I know how to live as the woman-on-her-own, how to do the daily mothering of sons, how to live on very little without feeling deprived, how to cope with the challenges of noise and pollution and the fast-paced life of the city. I know what it means to be the teacher in and leader of a small community of people committed to exploring their inner life.

The temptation, of course, is to identify with the new roles as quickly as possible and establish the package of reactions and responsibilities I think go with these roles. What does it mean to be a wife? Do I acquiesce gracefully to the role of homemaker, cleaning up after another adult for the first time in sixteen years, or do I decide on principle that Jeff must clean the toilet half the time whether it looks dirty to him or not? Given the incredible need of so many in the world, should I give away any income I do not need to cover immediate necessities? Or would saving be the prudent and responsible thing for a woman approaching fifty in uncertain economic times? Or would this reflect and exacerbate a basic lack of trust, an inability to live in the present? How much assistance should I give my sons? How often should I call them or ask them to come and visit? When am I trying to be overly involved in their lives, and when am I simply offering the support they need and deserve?

Questions about how to use our time and energy and resources, how to structure our relationships with our partner, families, and communities, are ones we all deal with. But most of the time we deal with them by creating a story for ourselves and our thoughts and feelings about the roles we play in these stories. Identifying with these stories, we unconsciously allow them to shape our decisions, to determine which of our constantly changing thoughts and feelings to act upon. It enables us to go on automatic pilot, gives us a sense—the illusion—of knowing who we are, of understanding ourselves. It allows us to go to sleep. The problem is not the stories we tell but our unconscious and often exclusive identification with these stories and the roles we assign ourselves within them.

I am in between stories. The old one is gone, and the new one is just beginning to take shape. When we already have a story we are heavily identified with, whether we appear to like this story or not, it is difficult to stay awake, to watch our thoughts and feelings without letting them dictate our actions. A clear story about who we are makes it hard to wait and let our actions arise from the deep and open emptiness of experiencing who we are right now, makes it difficult to allow actions to arise that may be inconsistent with how our story says we should move.

This time in between stories is happening for me just as menopause—another change, another gap in the story of who I am—begins to affect my physical, emotional, and mental sense of self. And I ask myself, who am I now that I am not the leader or teacher of a small community? Who am I now that my days are not dictated by the demands and challenges or buoyed up by the rewards of daily mothering? Who am I now that I do not have to come to terms—as I did sometimes gracefully and at other times with inelegant self-pity—with having few financial resources, with living in a large city, with meeting the challenges of being alone?

And I find in this time of change that all the things I took to be me, all the roles and reactions and responsibilities and conditions I identified as my self, reveal no self at all. This convergence of so much change in a relatively short period of time shows me that these roles and their corresponding thoughts and feelings always were perpetually changing, even as some "I" that is beyond or behind them all remains constant. This in-between time is not a trial to be endured, although at times I admit I have found it difficult to simply stay with no story and no self. This emptiness at the center is not a bewildering loss to be outrun. This gap in my story allows me to see how I am not what I do, allows me to create and play within new stories, new roles, without identifying exclusively with them.

Who would you be if you did not do whatever you do every day? What if you experimented in ways that could do no harm to yourself or others, were soft where you are normally hard, tender where you feel you must draw a firm line, giving where you usually take, receiving where you have no expectation or habit of receiving? What if you played with this solid sense of self you have built up, said what you were thinking when you usually remain silent, were quiet where you always felt you needed to add something? How much of the story you have created do you mistake for who and what you really are? Do you believe it liberates you from daily decision making to focus on other things? How much does it confine you, dictate which thoughts and feelings you follow into doing?

Create a gap in your story and sit within the gap, sit in the emptiness of not knowing who or what you are until an awareness of your essential nature fills you. We think the call, that which beckons us away from identifying exclusively with these stories we create, comes and goes. But the truth is it is always there, it is the very ground of existence. What comes and goes is our ability to hear it, our willingness to let go of what we think we are so we can open ourselves to hearing that which calls us back to what we always have been. When we open to this constant call, we remember why we are here and allow this knowledge to create a new and fluid story colored with that knowledge and never mistaken for all of who we are.

Going back to sleep, exclusively identifying who we are by the story we and our culture have cocreated, and being unable to wake up to full awareness of who we are and why we are here can be painful. But we can learn a great deal from the moments when we lose the thread of awareness, can gain knowledge about how to alleviate suffering in ourselves and the world in our bid to find our way back home. Our failures open us to truly receiving the grace that gives us this existence so we can hear the voice of the Beloved that calls, as Rumi wrote, saying,

Come, come again and still again,
even if thou hast broken thy truth a thousand times.

Meditation to See the Story

Most of the time we are not even aware of the story we are allowing to define and shape our choices. Sometimes it helps to see ourselves from a distance, to consider ourselves in the third person if we want to see the set of assumptions we are allowing to shape our daily view of reality over and over again. Again, in this meditation we are simply seeking a greater level of consciousness about what is. We do not need to judge what we discover. We are not required to do anything with the information we gain except be with it.

Sit in a comfortable position. If you find writing helps the flow of creative imagination, make sure a pen and paper are nearby. Take three deep breaths, filling your body with oxygen and exhaling all tiredness or tension in your body. Let go of all expectations of what is to come, breathing them out with the exhale. Let the weight of your body drop down. Let your mind follow your breath, gently bringing it back to the movement of air in and out of your body when thoughts and feelings come.

Imagine you are writing a screenplay or novel based on your own life as it is right now. How would you describe the character of this story? Just start the sentence, "He is . . ." or "She is . . ." over and over again and see what comes. How does it change if you start with, "He is the kind of man who . . . " or "She is the kind of woman who . . ."? Repeat the phrase and see what comes, writing each down and moving on to the next.

Putting down the pen and paper, bring your attention back to your breath. Once again, take three deep breaths, inhaling deeply and exhaling completely. Sit for a few moments focusing on your breath. Then pick up the sheet of paper and read what you have written, as if it were written about someone else. As you read each piece of the description, ask yourself what assumptions you would make about such a person. For instance, I might describe myself as someone whose work is solitary, completing the phrase as, "Her work is solitary." What assumptions do I have about people who work in solitude? That they are quiet, introverted, and creative, perhaps even a little eccentric. As I move through the statements, I can see how my assumptions create a story about my life, a solid identity out of situations, roles, and feelings that are fluid and changing.

Seeing these assumptions clustered around the roles in your life, consider where they shape how you behave, how you present yourself to the world. What do my assumptions about what it means to work in solitude mean for me when I am feeling extroverted, noisy, ordinary, or uncreative? Can I leave room for feelings and behaviors that do not fit the story I am creating in my mind about who I am and what I do? Can I participate in this story consciously when I choose to but not let it dictate my choices?

This is a messy process. If it feels confusing, slow it down. Sit with the pieces of the story you tell yourself about your life, and wait for the unconscious assumptions to surface. Be aware of the thoughts and feelings you have about these assumptions, neither pulling away from them nor enthusiastically declaring them to be the Truth. Just be with what is, and breathe.

Eleven

Your Word

Remember, there is one word you are here to say with your whole being.
When it finds you, give your life to it. Don't be tight-lipped and stingy.

This morning, like most mornings I have spent in this
new home, I sit alone at the kitchen table surrounded
by the deep silence of midwinter. When I walk from
the house to the studio I pause, steaming mug of tea in one hand,
and am greeted by the impenetrable quiet of dark cedars surrounded by white snow. Nothing moves. There is no sound. The
wind has temporarily died, leaving the powdered snow packed
tight in high drifts around the house. When I take a break for
lunch I will strap on my snowshoes, as I have each day this week,
and walk into the forest, hoping to penetrate the silence, wanting
to absorb it into the pores of my skin, seeking some guidance from
its constancy and indifference.

Later, walking among the snow-covered white pines, I realize
that this is in part what I love about this land—its indifference to
me. It welcomes me on its own terms. The resurrected wind makes

the current temperature of twenty degrees below zero feel like forty below. Feeling the sting of the wind's icy breath on my cheek, I know there will be no room for mistakes today. This is life-threatening cold. A twisted ankle could be fatal. In a world where humans seem so bent on bending and often breaking the rest of nature to their will, in a life where I am too often warring with reality in a futile attempt to shape it according to what I want, it's good to bump up against things that will not let me pretend control where none exists, realities that are indifferent to my momentary preferences and changing desires. It lets me rest.

Freed from identifying with the story of the life I was living in the city and not yet identified with any story of my life in this new place, I experience all movement as wandering. It's as if all my default settings have been erased and I must consciously choose in each moment what action to allow or to simply sit still. I pray and write, meditate and write some more, go for a walk in the woods and return when the desire to once more let the words flow onto the page rises from deep within.

The surprising and somewhat disconcerting thing is that I am experiencing this sense of moment-to-moment spaciousness directing my creative work even though I have made and intend to keep a commitment to deliver a manuscript to my publisher within the next six weeks. Clearly, at other times when I have become driven and goal oriented, insisting that external obligations necessitate frantic movement when those who care about me are trying to get me to slow down, the real source of my drivenness has been internal and has had little or nothing to do with external expectations. It's not that this is a particularly new or earthshaking insight, only that this is the first time I am actually experiencing that it is true. Never before, in the face of commitments and obligations, have I felt there was any real choice but to keep doing.

When we stop fighting reality, what is and always has been true can feel at first less real than the illusions we have mistaken for reality and have been operating under for years.

It takes days of this, a week or more of feeling unsettled and distracted by the unfamiliarity of it all, before I can become completely still with this strange new and creative emptiness. But finally one morning, this morning, I am able to just be with the vast space opened up by not exclusively identifying with and unconsciously following the outline of a particular story about who I am. As I do my practice of prayer and meditation, I am fully present in every moment. Sitting still, without thought, just being completely present, I am unexpectedly overwhelmed with a tiredness that makes my head fall down onto my chest where I sit. I feel as if I have been shot by a tranquilizer gun. I have had a good night's sleep and have been awake for only two hours, so I cannot understand this sudden and overwhelming exhaustion, but I do not fight it. I crawl onto the couch in the studio and, covering myself with a blanket, fall into a deep sleep.

And I dream. I dream the circle of Grandmothers is around me in the studio where I am sleeping. One of them leans close and asks me, "What would you want to tell the mothers?" Instantly I see a group of women, all of them mothers, who were participants in a program I ran many years ago for a mental health agency. My heart aches, remembering their struggles with poverty, addiction, abuse, and mental illness. And as I watch them, the group grows to include others: women and men I have counseled and taught, friends and family, men and women and children I do not recognize from all around the world. And for each of them I feel an incredible love and a deep compassion for the places in their lives where they struggle and suffer. My chest aches with a love that fills me like a bright light whose brilliance leaks out around my edges and makes my body translucent, threatening to split me open.

"What would you tell them?" the Grandmother whispers in my ear, leaning closer. As she speaks she reaches out one strong wrinkled hand and, grasping my shoulder, begins to rock my body back and forth on the bed as if to gently shake the answer to her question out of the wisdom my body holds. The movement is comforting, and I feel myself relaxing, falling down into a deeper level of sleep.

And there on the edge of the sweet oblivion of dark and dreamless sleep I whisper back to the Grandmother, "I would tell them to rest."

I have known for a long time that if there were one word I was here to contribute to the collective life, one word I was here to both learn to embody and teach, it would be *rest*. I didn't want this to be my word. I wanted my word to be something like *joy* or *laugh* or *create*. I knew from the beginning that it could not be *truth* or *beauty* or *love* or *peace*. These words are essence words, the words all of us are here to return to. Our individual words are smaller words, are about the ways in which particular human beings learn to live and embody truth and beauty and love and peace.

Of course this is just a story I tell myself, that each of us is here to say one word in the way we live our lives, in the choices we make. It's not a fact, although it might be the truth. It's a way of seeing my life, a way of opening to the call to live the meaning embedded in my life without feeling overwhelmed by the desire to do it all. For if we are all called to wake up to the sacred wholeness we are, we are also all called to live that wholeness in a particular way in the world given our own ego strengths and weaknesses, our own patterns of thoughts and feelings and sensations.

So ask yourself this: If I could say one word to the world, if I knew the world was listening attentively and would to the best of its ability follow the directive this word sent out, what would that word be? And then, instead of trying to think of the word, open yourself to seeing all the places in your life where the word you were meant to embody has been calling to you. Because it has. From the day you were born, one word has been calling to you, begging you to be with it, to learn the unique way in which only you could hold and embody and teach this word to the world. We think that the call, our vocation, will direct us in what to do with our lives. But I think the call tells you where you must begin to practice the not-doing that will allow the one word you are here to embody fill you and shape your life.

While I was working on this manuscript I decided to share the opening prose poem with some of the people who had written to me about my previous books. When they read "The Call" several wrote back baffled, expressing their frustration at this particular part of the poem. Why hadn't I told them what the word was? How were they going to find it? A few were angry, felt enticed by the promise that there was a specific reason they were here, only to have that reason withheld. I suspect some thought it was some kind of marketing technique intended to get them to buy the book. I couldn't help but imagine setting up workshops and charging outrageous sums of money promising to tell people their word, the specific way in which the meaning in their lives was to be lived. The frightening thing is that there would probably be more than a few people willing to sign up and pay for such a workshop.

So, let me be clear: *I don't know what your word is.* No one but you can find it. But I can tell you where to look. Look at your failures, at the places where you most easily go to sleep and become unconscious about what you are doing. Look at what does not come easily to you, what you long for but find elusive. Think about what gets you into trouble, what gets you way down the road of doing something you don't really want to do at a very high price. What internal habit or attitude or tendency repeatedly robs your life of joy?

You can feel how starting with your struggles and failures goes against the tendency of many New Age philosophies to start by looking at what you love and are good at. Why is your word not something you can easily do well, something that comes naturally to you? Because we cannot teach what we never had to learn, and we learn most where we have to stay conscious in order to learn.

Years ago I watched my friend Liza teach a class on bodywork. Liza is a talented hands-on healer, a practitioner of a multitude of bodywork techniques. Her training in these areas merely augments her natural intuitive ability to sense where and how to touch another's body to facilitate healing. She was a terrible bodywork teacher. When students would ask her how to know when to continue or stop a particular technique she would pause, grow flustered, and respond, "Well . . . you just know!" This was not helpful to the students. Most of them did not just know or at least had no way of recognizing what this knowing would look or feel like in themselves. Liza just knew, and because she had always had this ability she could not break it down and explain the steps, the pitfalls, the ways of finding this knowing if and when it was lost.

The best teachers are those who have had to carefully and consciously learn how to do the thing they are teaching. I have never and probably will never find myself unconsciously resting. My weakness in this area so fundamental to learning to live and love fully means I must be deliberately aware and conscious in order to rest. Years ago, ill with chronic fatigue syndrome, I came to recognize that although I was often horizontal or doing something others would find restful, I was not in fact resting at all but was continuing to do, if not externally then certainly internally. I had to realize that I did not know how to rest. Then I had to accept that rest was necessary and learn how to identify the taste and color and scent of rest when I found it. I struggled with my fears about rest: the fear that if I ever truly rested I would simply never get up again; the fear that I was unworthy of rest, that I had to earn the right to rest; the fear that at moments grew to a conviction that rest was available to everyone else but me. All of these things I continue to learn.

But most important, I had to learn and accept that rest is one of the ways—my way—to say "Yes!" to life, to offer who and what I am to the world. This would be equally true of whatever word you are here to embody and so share with others. When you consciously embody your word, you allow the "Yes!" the Beloved has whispered in your ear from the beginning to wake you up to what you are and why you are here. Whatever your word is, it cannot help but be one of the infinite expressions of the sacred life force that fills and surrounds us, for nothing is left out of that wholeness. Your word is one portal, your most likely entrance, into the now, into a direct experience of the meaning embedded in what you are. Not living your word is how you block the entrance to what you long for most. Lived consciously, your word becomes the door into that which satisfies your deepest longing.

Sometimes it helps to talk with those who know and love you if you want to begin to explore what your word might be. Your friends often have a clearer picture of what you don't do well, can remember where they have seen you repeatedly struggle and fall.

Generally, my dear friend Alison is much better at resting than I am. She can hang out with others or putter around the house or go for a Sunday drive and achieve rest in a way that is truly mystifying to me. *Rest* is not her word. What she does not do well is trust. She is often preparing or strategizing to counter the anticipated detrimental effects of impending circumstances or others' actions that may or may not happen and may or may not do her harm. She pours her lifeblood into any task she participates in with others, going beyond what is or should be expected, seeking to prove to herself and others that she can be relied upon to do a good job. She does not trust that they will see this if she does not take extraordinary measures. On a deeper level Alison often anticipates that things will not work out well for her, does not trust that she is participating in the law of averages just like the rest of us, and that her essential self will truly be okay no matter what happens. As I find rest elusive, Alison finds trust in scant supply.

Jeff has an enormous amount of trust. He expects things to work out well, and even when they don't he usually manages to keep his perspective on what matters and what does not. He is also the most skilled person I know when it comes to finding rest, which is probably one of the reasons I am so drawn to be with him. He can stop midtask and take a nap, has a wide range of hobbies he can putter at endlessly that offer him rest and renewal, and seems to do all of these completely guilt free. What Jeff does not do well is say no—to anyone at any time about anything. His fear of confrontation and disagreement leaves him agreeing to pretty much anything anyone asks of him even when it is something he cannot or does not want to do. Jeff's word may be something like *noncompliance* or even *confrontation*. Or maybe his word is simply *no*.

I could tell you what I know about why these three words call to Alison, Jeff, and me, could tell you stories about our developmental years that seem to explain why I find rest difficult, why Alison does not trust easily, and why Jeff finds it so hard to say no. But although understanding how our struggles may have been cultivated by early woundings or lessons may help us avoid unnecessary and unproductive shame about our area of struggle, it doesn't really change anything. As I get older it seems to me that I came into this life not knowing how to rest, particularly vulnerable from the beginning to messages around me that did not create but reinforced my tendency to ceaselessly do. Perhaps this reinforcement simply upped the ante and made it more likely that I would someday heed the call of the word I needed to learn to embody. I don't know. I do know that while understanding your struggles may offer some clues as to how to embody your word, how to live your calling, this understanding is most available not by reviewing the past but by observing what happens within and around you in the present moment.

There is a temptation when you are playing with this idea—and I would suggest you approach this playfully instead of doggedly trying to hunt down your word—to think of a word that is a bit grand and lofty. You'll know that you have the right word for you because there will be a rather humbling sense of recognition. Here I am, best-selling author and international speaker on matters of spirituality, and my word is *rest!?* What does that mean exactly? Am I to stay home with my feet up, reading novels and eating chocolates in order to maximize my contribution to the world? Am I violating my purpose in life every time I accomplish something or take on a task?

Finding your word can be a little tricky, but living it can be even more confusing. As I have discovered, I could stay at home and accomplish little and still never really be resting. Resting for me is about stopping my endless quest to get it right, do it perfectly, earn my way, or change the way things are. I can rest only when I can be with how things are in this moment. This is true whether I am lying in bed or writing a chapter or sitting on an airplane headed for a speaking engagement. Of course, I have to be able to accurately assess my current physical, mental, and emotional limitations, have to accept and monitor how fast I can move without moving away from the stillness that is deep within and all around me. But mostly, to rest I have to stop following the impulse to do in the hopes of changing the way things are.

Living your word, embodying it in your life, in how you are with yourself and the world, is never about doing. It is always about not-doing, about being with what is. Your word is your key to stopping your war with reality. The question becomes not so much how can I rest (and here you could put any word), but what must be surrendered, stopped, to allow rest (or your word again) to enter my life and live through me? What's the thread of thoughts and feelings I need to stop following into doing, opting instead to simply be?

For Alison, living her word means she must sit with her fear and not follow it into strategizing, plotting, and preparing for anticipated attacks or misfortune. Hostile actions by others may at times be what is, but whether or not the threat is real, following her fear into doing blocks the trust she needs to learn and live fully. When she sits with what is and waits for movement to come from her still center, she remembers what is real—that what she is at the deepest level of her being can never truly be harmed.

To live his word, Jeff has to learn to stop himself from agreeing to what others—even his outspoken wife—want the minute any request is made. When he sits with his fear of disappointing others and the confrontation he anticipates will follow, when he sits still with himself—even when others' disappointment or anger comes at him—without moving, without trying to make it okay, he is able to find his own still center more easily and let his choices, his movement, come from this essential core.

In all cases, living your word, stopping the habitual doing that is driven by fear, necessitates slowing things down, buying yourself some time in order to give yourself half a chance at consciously choosing something else, consciously choosing to embody your word. Consciously choosing to trust when the voice of fear is screaming and piling up evidence that others are untrustworthy, saying no when the voice of terror is pointing to the inevitable confrontation it is sure will do irrevocable harm to the self or the other if compliance is not offered instantly, finding rest when the internal voices are listing the three hundred things that simply have to be done immediately if disaster is to be averted—these things are not easy. And most often the voice of fear fueled by a life-and-death urgency sounds very reasonable, sounds as if it is simply and realistically telling us what is.

Living your word opens the door your fear has closed. Not doing what our fear for years has prompted us to do requires a certain level of consciousness. You have to be awake to know what is going on inside you.

I am not suggesting that those things that come easily to you are not part of the incredible gift you offer to the world. Liza's bodywork is one such gift to the world. Neither am I suggesting that you have to suffer in living your word. Rather, learning to live and embody your word will in fact alleviate a great deal of the suffering in your life and in the lives of those around you. My sons would be all too happy to testify to how my inability to rest has caused suffering in my life and theirs over the years, particularly when I have driven myself to the point of irritation, exhaustion, and long-term illness. Living your word does not cause suffering. Not living your word does.

The call is about finding the one thing you came here to say and saying it a thousand different ways—in your words, your actions, your choices—so you and the world can really hear it. It's about finding the end of the one thread that glows luminescent for you and following it faithfully to the time and place—here and now—where you can weave it into the fabric of your life and so offer it to the world. It's not about getting it right, not about living your word perfectly. It's about coming into lifelong relationship with the one word you long to know, the one word that seems at times to come so easily to others and yet has eluded you for most of your life. Out of our willingness to learn from our weakness, we develop a strength we can offer to others.

What if this was all that was required to live the meaning embedded in our lives, just this one thing: to embody in your life one word for all the world to hear; to explore the full depth and range of this word, its infinite manifestations and the equally infinite resistances you or others might have to living it; to let this word have its say through you so that the world might know it in a new way, in a way it could only be spoken through the particular blend of ego and essence that you are in this lifetime? What if I ate my meals, did my work, decorated my home, chose my clothing, interacted with friends and strangers in a way that manifests the full depth of the meaning of the word *rest?* I would eat, slowly and lightly, whole foods that would let my body replenish and my digestive system rest. I would intersperse my work—at home or on the road—with short walks, soft music, and long naps. I would decorate my home in colors that are restful to the eye, creating spaces that support slowing down to look out a window or stare at a fire burning in the hearth. I would wear comfortable clothing that did not require me to pull myself up out of tiredness to hold in stomach muscles—silk pajamas and warm flowing skirts that tuck easily around legs pulled up onto comfortable chairs or chaise lounges. I would see the tiredness in myself and others, even when it is disguised as rage or judgment or self-pity, and touch this tiredness gently, giving permission in the tone and speed and volume of my words, in the way I hold my body and interact with others, for us all to rest. I would seek to embody restfulness, knowing that when I do it ripples out from me and touches all those around me, and beyond them all those in the world. I might make my dedication to rest explicit in the work I do with others, offering retreats where others can find rest and learn ways to consciously cultivate it in their lives. But this is not a necessary prerequisite for embodying my word, and in fact it brings with it the risk that I will make resting another project to be mastered. There can be no separation between means and ends. I cannot teach rest while abandoning it for myself. It is less what I do than how I am that will determine whether or not I am embodying the essence of my word and so sharing it with the world.

We are a tired people, and it is hard for tired people to sit still and let the wisdom they need find them. Rest is necessary if we are to have the heart and energy to remain conscious, if we are to be able to see and not unconsciously identify with and follow into action our fears from the past or our fears for the future, if we are to be in the now. But it is equally true that we need the trust that Alison can embody for the world, trust in our essential nature, our innocence, trust in that which is larger than ourselves, in the flow of the sacred life force to take us all home. And it is also true that we need boundaries, need to be able to say no to what does not feed us or our children, what does not create beauty for ourselves or the world, if we are to be true to what we are.

The infinite ways in which we can embody the words that call to us are a mirror of the interbeingness of reality. The power of each word, its ability to take us back to the home we long for, to the awareness of what we are and why we are here, is awakened when it is consciously realized. The possibilities are infinite: *choose, stop, listen, answer, give, wait, receive, play, begin, finish, enough, value, discard, preserve, mother, sister, brother, father, release, hold, discern, nourish, prune, evaluate, accept, jump, laugh, cry, grieve, rejoice, pray, shout, whisper, dance, speak. . . .* There is nothing left out, nothing that cannot be included, but each of us does not have to do it all. We just have to do our part, and our part is to give ourselves completely to the word that has called out to us all our lives. And in the moments when you can't yet give yourself completely to this word, choose to give yourself completely to your struggle with this word. When I cannot rest, I can be with my tiredness and my struggle to find rest. When Alison cannot trust, she can consciously be with her feelings of distrust, can simply sit with her fear that something or someone may do her harm. When Jeff cannot say no, he can be aware of his feeling of being trapped into compliance, his discomfort with confrontation and conflict. When we can be with our inability to let the word we know is ours guide us, we soften to ourselves and to our struggle, and the word begins to enter.

So don't hold back. When you find your word, when you are willing to let it find you—and you can hear it only here and now—give your life, this moment, to it. Let it guide what you do and how you do it, let it shape your choices and color your visions. Because the word that calls to you is not only what you need to go home to an awareness of what you are. It is the word the world needs you to embody so we can all go home together. It is God speaking to you, through you. It is what you are here to say.

Meditation on Your Word

If you are like me, you could make finding and embodying your word a whole new project, something to get right, something more to do. That won't work. You have to let your word find you. You have to listen for the ways in which it is calling to you and has been calling to you all your life. You can put yourself in the place of listening, but it may take awhile before you can silence your eagerness or anxiety enough to hear. On the other hand, what you are here to offer to the world may be the first word that popped into your consciousness when you first casually wondered about this idea. Of course, if you are like me, you will assume that anything that came so easily couldn't possibly be accurate and devote yourself to hours of sitting in meditation to make sure you have it right. Be gentle with yourself. The word you are here to embody has been whispered to you by the Beloved from the moment you entered this life. Just let yourself be, and you will hear it reverberate through your heart.

And ask.

Sit in a comfortable position and take three deep breaths, letting yourself settle into your position and come into the present moment fully with your breath. Let your shoulders drop and your weight sink down, being aware of the surface that supports you. Let the exhale gently release all tiredness and tension from your body. If any thoughts or feelings come during this time, allow them to simply slip away like pearls on silk, bringing your attention back to your breath.

Be present. Be with your breath and your body and your surroundings. Keep most of your attention focused on each exhale, but do not try to block out the sounds or smells or sight of things around you. Just be.

When you are ready, allow one thought to form. You may wish to make it a question: "What is the word I am here to say for myself and my people?" You may wish to make it a request: "Tell me the word I am here to embody for myself and the world." Ask, and then wait without waiting. Listen without straining. If a word comes, sit with it, breathe it into your body, and see what truth it holds for you. Do you recognize it as a word you have found difficult to live, a word you have longed to know and embody, a word that pulls you toward waking up? Do not judge what comes, even if what comes is silence. Be with yourself, and let the word find you. You will recognize it when it does.

Twelve

Together

Spend yourself completely on the saying.
Be one word in this great love poem we are writing together.

The voice leaving a message on my answering machine is familiar and filled with anguish. Alarmed, I lean forward, wanting to catch every word.

"Oriah . . . it's Catharine. I . . . I think I screwed up." Her voice breaks. "I am so sorry. I . . . I don't know what to do."

Catharine is a dear friend. Nine years ago, while visiting my home, she had a brain aneurysm burst. On the way to the hospital her heart stopped beating and she stopped breathing and had to be revived several times. After five weeks in a coma she woke up, recognized her mother and me, did not recognize her husband or remember how to use a spoon, a toothbrush, or a comb, could not tie her own shoes or walk unassisted. Since that time she has been living in a group home for people with acquired brain injuries. That's what they call it, "acquired brain injuries." It sounds as if a purchase has been made. If so, Catharine did not get the better end of that bargain.

Over time, with a great deal of work and perseverance, Catharine has regained some of her memories. She can walk slowly and do simple tasks like feed herself and brush her teeth. Although she will never be able to live independently, she has remained doggedly optimistic, telling me frequently and with absolute determination that she intends to live a long life and that she is going to continue to heal and improve. She seems genuinely happy to be alive, always overtly grateful for the small things—the warmth of the sun, the kindness of those who care for her, the taste of good food.

But now Catharine is struggling. Over the last few months her physical health and mental acuity have declined sharply. She is often too tired to participate in the activities the staff at the group home arrange for her. Her mind has become confused, sometimes not recognizing people who were familiar to her, often forgetting things she has known. Her emotional affect is periodically flat, strangely detached as it was when she first came out of the coma. The director of the group home wonders if she may have dementia or Alzheimer's, conditions that sometimes appear prematurely in people with serious brain injuries.

Speaking with her on the phone now, I hear Catharine's words slow and slurred, as they often are these days. She is upset because someone in the group home has asserted that there is no divine presence, no God or Great Mystery. I wonder, if I'd had my life as I'd known it—my memories and ability to function in the world—taken from me, if I would find it hard to believe that there was no Beloved who cares for us. Catharine is upset because she feels she did not do an adequate job during an argument the night before defending her belief in something greater than herself. Because I had been her spiritual teacher for many years, she feels in some way she has betrayed me or the teachings and practices I have shared with her. It breaks my heart to hear her so distraught. It is the first time I have heard her in agony about her declining abilities.

"I tried, Oriah," she says. "I tried so hard to tell him what I knew about the Mystery, but I couldn't hang onto the thoughts, I couldn't find the words, I couldn't be clear." Her voice rises in desperation. "I really screwed up. Will the Mystery forgive me?"

"Oh, Catharine, it's okay. Please don't. You don't have to defend what you know. The Mystery doesn't care about arguing well." I pause, trying to reach for some lightness, and remember a Sufi story I once heard Coleman Barks tell. "It's like fish arguing about the existence of water." She laughs weakly, clearly relieved. "You sound tired, Catharine."

"I am," she says. "I am very tired." In the pause I hear her take a deep breath. "I have tried my hardest, Oriah. You know that, don't you? You know I have tried to do my best since all this happened to me?"

"Yes, Catharine. I know you have tried very hard." I wait for the words to come and then say softly and slowly, "Catharine, you don't need to try so hard. You need to rest now. You don't have to try so hard to hang on. You can let go, and let it be the way it is."

We sit and listen to the hum of silence on the telephone line, my face wet with tears. I was Catharine's teacher when I knew nothing of letting go, when by my actions if not my words I pushed myself and all those around me to try harder, work longer, and never let go. I want Catharine to hear a different message from me now, to know as I know now that we do not earn the Beloved's embrace, that answering the call to live fully is more about surrendering to simply being than continuing our doing.

Her voice is small, hesitant, and sounds younger than her fifty-three years. "I'm thinking . . . I'm thinking of asking Mum and Dad to take me on a trip . . . maybe a boat tour."

My breath catches, but I struggle to keep my voice even. Catharine's father has been dead for over fifteen years. Her mother is elderly and very ill.

"I think that's a good idea, Catharine, if that's what you want."

She pauses. "You do know my father is dead?" she asks.

"Yes, I remember."

Silent for a few moments, each of us sits with the implications of this. Is it possible Catharine is telling me she is dying or that she wants to die?

"Thank you," she says slowly, "for being so . . . soft with me."

"I love you, Catharine. Whatever happens, wherever we are, we will always be connected to each other. You are my sister."

"Yes," she says quietly, "I know that." There is another long pause before she continues. "I think maybe I should do what you are suggesting. I think maybe I should rest now."

We say good-bye and hang up.

The shift in my life that instigated the writing of the first book in this trilogy, *The Invitation,* started with Catharine's brain aneurysm. The prose poem was written exactly one year from the day Catharine complained of a sharp pain in her head while standing in my kitchen. *The Invitation* was the long, low wail of my heart opened to its own longing by the harsh reality of being unable to save someone I loved from pain and suffering. That wail reminded me of what mattered and what did not, of my deep ache for rest and intimacy, needs I had tried to leave behind. Our longing may be just the beginning, just a door into a deeper knowledge of what we are and why we are here, but it is a necessary beginning. We cannot go deeper into our lives or the world until the heart has had its say, until the heart has been heard.

After the brain aneurysm, after it was clear that Catharine's life would never be the same, she asked me to make all she had been through "count," to learn something from it all and share it with others. So I followed the thread of my longing into the quest to learn how to live the soul's desires, writing *The Dance*. And I discovered that the way to live the soul's desires was not to try and change who I was but to become who I was on the deepest level of my being, to allow who I was to unfold. But sometimes, when you have been folded in many places for a long time, unfolding can be painful and hard. As I wrote, Catharine surpassed the doctors' expectations, working to restore her mind and body, struggling to remember how to walk and sit and lift a fork, laboring to piece together a life surrounded by caregivers and strangers brought together by shared challenges to live in the same house. We both worked hard, although Catharine's task was by far the more difficult, each of us trying in our own way to make what had happened count, trying to stay awake in order to learn what we could, trying to be worthy of the lessons we were learning. Each of us kept trying to do it right, fueled by our desire to change what was—Catharine striving to do all that she could to beat the effects of the brain aneurysm, I struggling to do whatever it would take to live true to the soul's deepest desires.

One day you wake up and realize that doing is simply not what is required. It wouldn't be accurate to say that what either of us had done wasn't enough. That would imply that there might have been something else we could have done if we had just tried harder. But for each of us, what we longed for—living life fully in a way that would make all we had learned "count"—could not be achieved by doing. On some level deep within, each of us knows this and is called to remember what we know. I wondered after our telephone conversation if Catharine telling me about wanting to take a trip with her parents was similar to my mind's eye's offering me an image of myself with my hands severed: the psyche's way of declaring, "I quit." Because the cost of doing, of taking action fueled by our resistance to what is and our overwhelming attachment to changing it, is a diminishing ability to live and love fully, to be in the now, to be at peace, to know who and what we are and so experience the meaning enfolded in simply being.

I have reached a place where my longing to live the meaning in my life is greater than my fear of letting go of doing. Perhaps Catharine, in her own way, has also reached this place. I wanted what I said to her, how I was with her, to give her whatever she needed to stop doing, whatever she needed to allow herself to simply be. Of course, the degree to which I can do this, the effectiveness of my words, is directly proportional to the degree to which I am able to simply be with myself and the world as it is right now.

Human beings love the story of the hero, the one who does the impossible, who saves the other by doing what no one else could do. But what happens when doing is not what is required? After September 11, I heard stories of New York firefighters who were considering quitting their jobs. When I was in New York I began to understand why it might be hard for these men to continue. Firefighters are trained to be heroes, to go in and do what no one else can. And they did. They walked up the stairs of the burning World Trade Center, carrying heavy equipment and reassuring those who were descending, courageously following the procedure set for high-rise fires even though they knew this was beyond the scope of anything they had ever encountered. And after the towers fell those who were left dug through the rubble for days and nights searching for survivors. They did what they had been trained to do. And it didn't make much of a difference. No amount of doing could significantly change things. Climbing the stairs could not prevent the building from collapsing. There were too few survivors to find and rescue.

When we have put our faith in doing, where do we turn when there is simply nothing to be done that can make a difference? This is hard for everyone but harder, I think, for men because boys are taught to believe more deeply in the power of their ability to make what is wrong right with what they do, and harder for Americans who have built a flourishing nation and a powerful mythology on a philosophy of heroic action. I am not suggesting that great things are not at times achieved by the hero's actions. Often lives are saved by someone's self-sacrificing deeds, although the truth is that the one who reaches out for another, risking his or her own life to do so, is probably acting more from the impulse that springs from the depth of being fully present than from any misguided faith in doing.

Learning to stay connected to an awareness of our essential stillness does not mean we will remain immobile when movement is required. The impulse to move will be there when that movement will truly serve life on the deepest level. Not-doing is not about immobility or giving up in despair. It is first and foremost about being able to be with, to accept fully, what is in this moment. Catharine may continue to take action that will expand her abilities, but I suspect she can no longer take this action from the place of doing, from rejecting what is and wanting to change it, because she is simply worn out.

When the hero sits down, face in hands, back bowed by the weight of what cannot be done, who can help him or her be with what is in a way that does not crush us all? The one who is able to be with the self and the world. Telling someone to rest, to stop doing, while you are racing by and doing more is not effective. How we live with what is determines what ripples out into the world, determines whether or not our touching others will allow them to experience a moment of their own essential stillness and the peace and meaning this stillness holds.

To be with each other, to allow our lives together to declare our devotion to the meaning embedded in life itself, we have to be able to hear each other, to witness and appreciate the many ways that our essential nature is embodied in different human lives. We can choose to stay only with those who think and feel as we do, but how much richer our lives are if we can accept that the essence of what we are leaves nothing out, includes it all.

When I receive an invitation to meet with and speak to employees at NASA's space flight center near Washington, D.C., I wonder out loud if the invitation is a hoax. When it turns out to be genuine my son Nathan asks incredulously, "Do they know who you are?"

Slightly insulted, I retort, "No, I think they've mistaken me for the other Oriah Mountain Dreamer, the nuclear physicist!"

Nathan is undaunted. "What do you have to say to a group of scientists at NASA?"

His question echoes my own doubts, but I reply with all the confidence I can muster, "I'll say what I always say. Scientists are human beings like everyone else. They have the same struggles, the same questions about how to live life fully." Luckily, Jeff is a scientist, so I know this is true.

However, I also know that different groups of people, what we might call even in this world of global awareness "different tribes," express their questions and live their quest for meaning in different ways. Preparing to speak at NASA, I wonder how to translate my experience of my own spirituality in a way that will make sense to people of a different tribe, to people of a scientific tribe. And I think of when Jeff and I met.

We were teenagers on a canoe trip in Algonquin Park in central Ontario. Now, years later, Jeff tells me that at that initial meeting he deliberately jockeyed for a position on the outfitters dock that would ensure him a place in the same canoe as the outspoken, long-legged girl in the yellow shorts. So for the next two weeks we paddled and talked and argued with each other. One of the arguments I remember most clearly was about religion. I argued that all differences between religions did not amount to anything important, that the common experience of the vastness and love of the divine far outweighed the differences in how people approached or explained or celebrated this experience, and so there should be only one religion. Jeff, by contrast, argued that there should be as many religions as there were people because each person needed to find their own particular way into a sense of the sacred. We were both right, and although we did not have the language to speak about it then, we were talking not so much about religion, human beings' codified beliefs and rituals, but about spirituality, the direct experience of that which is larger than and yet deep within ourselves.

One of the ways that Jeff touches the sacred, that largeness in which we participate, is through astronomy. Even on that canoe trip thirty years ago he had with him a telescope he had made himself. When Jeff invited me to go out alone with him at night to see the constellations, I found, much to my disappointment, that he really meant to see the constellations. I had hoped for more romantic motivations. At the time I did not understand how naming the constellations was the way Jeff moved closer to the fire that was the source of what we both felt when we were together.

Jeff's knowledge of astronomy and his active involvement in building telescopes and charting the night sky open him to a sense of how vast and magnificent the universe is and how small—and magnificent—we are. The planets of our solar system orbit around the sun, one of the two billion stars in our galaxy, the Milky Way. This galaxy is one hundred thousand light-years in diameter (compared to the .02 light-seconds between New York and London) and is only one of the over thirty galaxies in what astronomers call our Local Group. The galaxy within this group that is closest to us, the Andromeda Galaxy, is two and a half million light-years away, and of course there are, for all practical purposes, an infinite number of groups of galaxies in the universe.

Once, explaining his passion for astronomy to me, he said, "I want to be able to look up at the night sky anywhere on this planet and know where I am." I knew when he said it that he wasn't referring to getting the kind of information a global tracking device could provide. And when I share his comment with the group of scientists I am having lunch with when I visit NASA, I can see in the murmur of instant understanding and the nodding heads around the table that they know what he means because it is the same for them. For these people, knowing where they are in the physical universe, concretely exploring and observing and charting the vastness of this immense creation, is what allows them to touch an awareness of who they are and why they are here. And as with all experiences of being fully with what is, the meaning found in the experience may be more implicit than explicit, but it is felt as that which gives direction and purpose to our lives.

To me, all that calculating and calibrating and building and moving of equipment just looks like too much work. But that's just because it's not my way. Recognizing your own tribe, those with whom you share a particular way of touching the mystery and living your essence, is important. But finding ways to speak to and appreciate each other's ways of knowing the Sacred Mystery is critical if we are to create a world that reflects the essence of that common experience and celebrates the beauty of the variety it nourishes. Our lives can only be made richer by expanding the number of ways we allow the Beloved to speak to us. We mistake rigid human-created categories for reality, but reality knows no mutual exclusivity. The most prevalent characteristic of my experience of that still and spacious ground of being at the center of what

I am is its inclusiveness. In this present moment—the only moment in which we can experience what we are—this essence excludes nothing that is, even those things the mind struggles to bring together. I run up against my own mind's prejudice when speaking at NASA, faltering slightly in the recitation of one of Rumi's poems about the Beloved, when I notice a man in the audience wearing a military uniform taking notes. Later, a woman from the United States Defense Department who was in the audience brings a pile of books to be signed, one for each of the people in her division. My mind struggles to put together what it has separated, to include again what I am tempted to see as not part of the wholeness of the Beloved.

The truth is that even when we are too tired or afraid to see the movement of the mystery around and within us, it is always there. Once in a while we are awake enough to see the ripple of the sacred emptiness that holds it all when it comes toward us from another.

I am walking through an underground mall on my way to the subway a week before Christmas. I am late for an appointment and so am walking quickly, making my way around shoppers who are proceeding at a more nonchalant pace. Suddenly the oncoming crowd grows dense as a group of people emerges from the subway, and I am caught behind a woman who is walking with three small boys, each around five years old. She holds the hands of two of them, and the third holds the hand of the child to her left. They are sauntering, bouncing along in oversized snow boots with small erratic movements, their mittens trailing from strings in the sleeves of their unzipped jackets. With the oncoming pedestrian traffic there is simply no way to get around them. I feel my impatience and, taking a breath, let it go, slowing my pace to walk behind them. The boys are looking at the store windows lining the underground passageway, eyes wide with amazement at the lights and tinsel and decorations, pointing excitedly at an animated Santa or a huge stuffed stocking. Suddenly one of the boys breaks into song, singing "Jingle Bells" at the top of his lungs, never taking his eyes away from the windows he is passing. The other two pick up the song, their high, small voices echoing off the low ceiling of the underground passageway.

Another surge of pedestrians emerges from the subway and moves toward us quickly, carrying briefcases and backpacks, looking weary and impatient in their rush to get home. I watch as the crowd approaches, as they begin to see and hear the boys ahead of me singing at the top of their lungs. One by one the men and women barreling along after a long day at work slow their pace and start grinning. It's like a wave rolling through the approaching crowd. The boys are oblivious to the effect they are having. Completely unselfconscious, they keep their eyes glued to the glittering windows they are passing. They are not trying to garner approval or attention. The song bursts from their small bodies the way chirping does from the fat round chickadees that sit in the tree outside my bedroom window every morning, singing the sun up as if their lives depended upon it.

I realize, watching these boys and the effect that their singing—the movement that is spontaneously arising from being in this moment—is having on everyone around them, that our lives do depend upon it, that our lives individually and collectively depend upon our willingness to be available to the song that wants to burst forth from us. The degree to which we are present and available to the divine presence within and around us in this moment determines what will ripple out from us into the world. When I ask, "If you knew the world were listening attentively, what is the one word you would say?" I want to remind us all that the world *is* listening, all the time. How we are ripples out from us into the world and affects others. We have a responsibility—an ability to respond—to the world. Finding our particular way of living this responsibility, of offering who we are to the world, is why we are here. We are called because the world needs us to embody the meaning in our lives. God needs us awake. This world we live in is a cocreation, a manifestation of individual consciousness woven into a collective dream. How we are with each other as individuals, as groups, as nations and tribes is what shapes that dream.

My dear friend Mickey Lemle makes films that send out ripples of awareness into this collective dream. The effect of a scene in his latest movie, *Fierce Compassion,* has stayed with me since I saw it. In this scene Dr. Larry Brilliant, cofounder of the SEVA foundation, a charitable foundation promoting community service, recounts a story of traveling to India to meet and sit with Maharaj-ji, guru to the American spiritual teacher Ram Dass. Speaking of the incredible love Maharaj-ji had for everyone, Larry tells us, "I could almost begin to understand how he loved everybody. I mean, that was sort of his job. He was a saint. Saints are supposed to love everybody. That's not what has always staggered me. What staggered me is not that he loved everybody, but that when I was sitting in front of him I loved everybody."

This is the effect that ripples out from someone who is fully awake to what we all are: those in proximity wake up and experience the divine spark that lives within themselves. And this awareness ripples out from them to touch others. There is no way to fake this. We can talk endlessly about deep stillness and the sacred presence within and around us, but talk will never get us there because there is nowhere to get to and what we are is beyond thinking and words. Doing will not take us there, either, because doing is always at least a little about pulling away from what is, while being—that still, spacious whole presence that you are, that everything is—is about accepting fully and being with what is here and now. When we hold this place, if only for a moment, our very presence creates a similar response in others to all that is in this moment, saying, "Yes!"

When I surrender to simply being fully here and now with whatever is in this moment, with my own thoughts and feelings and sensations, with the way things are around me and in the world, not pulling away from or grasping at what is but simply being with it, I hear the call that speaks to me and through me, whispering the truth each of us has always known. And I pick up my pen and write what I hear:

> *There is nowhere to rest your eye*
> *that does not behold the face of the Beloved.*
> *There is nothing here but you and God,*
> *and no real harm can ever be done to either,*
> *so what is there to forgive?*
> *Ah, it's so hard to keep this perspective,*
> *to remember the truth when things get crazy*

and we fear the worst.
All I can do is go back to my breath
and remember that the Holy Spirit
is what fills me with every inhale.
How could it be otherwise?
When we get it, all this anguish seems so unnecessary.
When we lose it, suffering seems to be the only option.
All things have their roots planted in the same sacred soil.
Nothing is excluded from the sacred ground of being.
What would happen if we could remember this?
What place would be unsuitable for a shrine?
Brothel or barn, crack house or cathedral: all sacred.
What person would not be another yourself,
a shining and holy face of the Sacred Mystery?
Remember this when you look at those you call your enemies.
Even your darkest secrets,
the things about your self that make you cringe—
do you think the sacred presence is not large enough to include these?
How small our notion of God is.
How our ideas fail to even guess at the depth of the passion
the Beloved feels for us.

Open your eyes.
See, there is nothing here but you and the Beloved,
and no real separation between even these two.

Now that ought to make you smile.

—Oriah Mountain Dreamer

Meditation on Simply Being

In the end there is nowhere to go, nothing to do, there is only being and the infinite movement of life that flows from the deep stillness at the center of all that is. Awareness of your essential nature, waking up to what you are, begins with the willingness to be with what is. There is no trick, no complex methodology. There is only the practice of bringing yourself to the present moment and being with all that present moment holds.

Sit in a position that is comfortable. Sometimes it helps to dedicate your formal time of being present to what you love—to say a small prayer that declares your intent, that reminds you why you are here. Do this as you begin. Let the longing of your heart guide your words. If you are in a place where you are comfortable doing so, speak the words out loud, let them reverberate in the world. What brings you here? To what do you dedicate this time of simply being? Do you have a request of the stillness?

What do you want to ripple out from you as you sit in the present moment?

Take three deep breaths in through your nose and out through your mouth, letting your body rise with the inhale and fall with the exhale. Let your body drop down, supported by the surface beneath it. Let any resistance to what is in this moment move out with the exhale. Let yourself be fully present, aware of your body and your surroundings, bringing most of your attention to your breath as it moves in and out of your body. Allow yourself to sit and be with whatever is within and around you. As thoughts and feelings and sensations come, simply notice them briefly and gently let them go, bringing your attention back to your breath. Feel yourself sink down deeper into less and less doing and more and more awareness of simply being here now. Open. Let all things be as they are in this moment.

Acknowledgments

To my agent, Joe Durepos, a truly good man.

To the diligent team at Harper San Francisco who bring it all together with style and grace: publisher Stephen Hanselman, editor John Loudon, Margery Buchanan, Calla Devlin, Kris Ashley, Priscilla Stuckey, Jim Warner, and Chris Hafner.

To Martha and Todd Lucier of Northern Edge Algonquin, for their hospitality and tender care.

To the friends who listen to my stories and offer me their own: Jude Cockman, Cat Scoular, Judith Edwards, Philomene Hoffman, Liza Parkinson, Diana Meredith, Peter Marmorek, Wilder Penfield, Ingrid Szymkowiak, Linda Mulhall, Lise Tetrault, Joan Borysenko, Christina Vander Pyl, Catherine Mloszweska, Ellen Martin, Mark Kelso, Thom Rutledge, Mickey Lemle, Ann Petrie, Judy Crawford-Smith, and Elizabeth Verwey.

To my parents, Don and Carolyn House, for their continued loving support.

To my sons, Brendan and Nathan, who are always challenging me and cheering for me at the same time.

To my husband, Jeff, who walks beside me.

To the Sacred Mystery that never stops calling my name, even when I'm not listening.
Thank you.

For information about Oriah Mountain Dreamer's
publications and book tours, go to:
www.oriahmountaindreamer.com

or write to:
300 Coxwell Avenue
P.O. Box 22546
Toronto, ON
Canada
M4L 2AO